ADULT EDUCATION

Lyman Bryson

PROFESSOR OF EDUCATION
TEACHERS COLLEGE
COLUMBIA UNIVERSITY

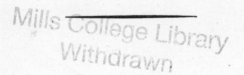
NEW YORK CINCINNATI CHICAGO
AMERICAN BOOK COMPANY
BOSTON ATLANTA DALLAS SAN FRANCISCO

Copyright, 1936, By
AMERICAN BOOK COMPANY

BRYSON'S ADULT EDUCATION

W. P. I

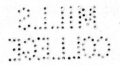

Made in U.S.A.

PREFACE

WRITING a textbook in a new field is a dangerous venture. Words have a way of looking final when they get into print. An author may protest, as the writer of this book wishes emphatically to protest, that his conclusions are all tentative. He will still be suspected of assuming authority. But there are thousands of students of the social scene and of education in America who have been wanting a systematic account of adult education and this book was written to be of service to them. If it helps them ask the right questions of their own experience and to work out their own philosophy and methods, it will have done all that could be hoped for it.

The material here presented, although tentatively used, was gathered in the course of considerable work in the field in the promotion and administration of programs, in the leading of adult groups, and in training prospective leaders.

The book owes a great deal to many colleagues and students with whom problems have been discussed. Special thanks are gratefully recorded: to Mrs. Lucy Wilcox Adams for long association in thinking out these problems and attempting to solve them in practice; to Miss Dorothy Rowden and Professor Edmund deS. Brunner for reading the first draft and making many useful suggestions; and to Miss Katherine McGrattan for help in preparing the manuscript.

iii

CONTENTS

ADULT EDUCATION

Chapter One

WHY GO ON LEARNING?

LIFELONG learning is an ancient ideal in the history of civilization, but adult education as an organized social movement is comparatively new in American life. It is not new for great teachers to address their words to mature minds; they have always done that since the days of Buddha and Socrates. And many now active agencies have had a long and honorable history. The great importance of the movement at present is due to the increasing co-operation between public and volunteer agencies for the general betterment of the intellectual climate of the United States. This has been going on for not much more than a decade. Pressure and change in modern life have made it necessary for civic leaders to take stock of opportunities for self-education and to help men and women to continue their personal development.

The words "adult education," being fashionable, are now used to cover a multitude of activities. Many are commercial, as when advertising undertakes to "educate" the people to buy some product of mass fabrication. Without drawing any invidious distinction, the term will be applied here only to activities that are not primarily for profit. We can define adult education as including all the activities with an educational purpose that are carried on by people engaged in the ordinary

3

business of life. Age alone will not suffice to mark off the limits of its clientele. A man pursues a doctor's degree at the age of 30. He is an "adult" in age. But he is only continuing in the school system. He is not in any real sense a seeker after "adult education." On the other hand, a boy of 16, recently graduated from high school, continues on his own initiative to enrich his background or refine his occupational skill. He is genuinely in the movement. Getting a necessary schooling is the child's "business." An adult is one who has other business in the world but who uses part of his time and energy to acquire more intellectual equipment.

We are helped toward an understanding of the spirit of the movement if we think of all adult education as voluntary. Self-direction is its most characteristic quality. It is true that certain types of training, such as those designed to cure illiteracy, or to give underprivileged men and women a minimum initiation into citizenship, may be compulsory. But for the most part adult students seek further learning because of self-determined needs, because in the actual working out of their lives they find further learning necessary and desirable. And the love of learning for its own sake is strong in the motives of thousands of people who are innocent of scholarly distinction.

No society can exist without education as a consciously managed institution. Man differs from other animals largely by reason of the fact that his environment extends beyond his immediate experience both in time and in place. Modern man lives in a world which includes, as "environment," a great deal of all that has ever been thought and felt by the other men who have occupied the earth since the beginning of language and cultural accumulation. There is no scientific evidence for the natural notion that a child is born with special aptitudes for the culture in which he is to live. He is born a human being; he is made into a Frenchman or a Russian or a Chinese by processes which begin to bear heavily upon him from the moment of birth. He acquires language, ideals, ways of doing things, skills, prejudices, and loyalties. If it were possible to imagine a human being separated from all this externally acquired culture, one might say that the infant could as easily have become a member of some other social group—if he had received the training of that group. Fundamental attitudes are no doubt acquired in infancy, but life is lived largely by the use of definitely learned symbols and skills, and before the age of seven, when a child normally enters school, he has not gone far in the acquisition of those tools. And education, even when we mean by that word only the organized school system, excluding all educating influences of home and companionship, still plays the largest part in transferring culture from one generation to another. Man lives in an environment which extends beyond his own experience in time and place because he lives for a while in a school. No change in social organization and no ambition on the part of educators will ever free education from responsibility as a special agency for rebuilding civilization afresh out of each new generation of raw materials.

As civilization develops, however, this culture which must be handed down by the school process becomes constantly less simple and less static. A society like our own is undergoing rapid change in industrial and social processes with a constant acceleration and complication. The primary task of handing down the social heritage becomes increasingly difficult. Even in historical times, through long centuries men moved very slowly from one change to another. Men did things much as their grandfathers had done them. They confidently expected their grandsons to do the same things in similar fashion. The manners and lore which the child needed to acquire were easily inculcated and the schooling, once acquired, could well serve through a lifetime. Similarly, the cultural material itself, for the vast bulk of the population at least, was simple. School years were short, partly because many things were learned by direct apprenticeship and from parental contacts, but also because the knowledge available for the general use was meager.

That education is no longer so simple or so static is evident to anyone who will compare what he himself learned in high school with what the present generation of high-school students is undertaking to learn. It is a commonplace but profoundly significant truth that any boy or girl in high school today knows more about the physical and chemical nature of the universe than his parents knew or could possibly have known when they were in high school or, in fact, than anyone knew twenty or thirty years ago. But even that very complicated and difficult acquaintance with the world which is now expected of young people in school will not suffice for a lifetime. More things are constantly being discovered. More things are constantly being invented. And it is because there is so much to be learned for anyone who wishes to be at home in the modern world, and because so little of it can be counted on to have validity over a long period of time that education can no longer be considered a terminal phase of life.

The very simple notion of getting an education and then going out into the world to use it no longer suffices. Learning becomes a necessary element in the life process, continuing as long as life itself continues. The conscious organization of adult education, that is, the provision of opportunities for continuing intellectual betterment, has become not merely desirable but necessary. Modern civilization cannot be given over to new generations of children and safely entrusted to them if they continue to work only with what they can learn in their first intense educational experience.

The transfer of culture to the child is not, however, the whole of the responsibility of education as a social agency. If it were all that is needed, and could be successfully achieved, society would stand still. Civilization may perhaps grow because of mystic forces hidden in the destinies of men. To our factual vision, it grows because men, for varying motives, do things that result in change. Without at all asserting that changes are largely rational or that there is any general social purpose in much of the manipulation of the social situation constantly going on, we can still say that change comes because men desire it. Men are discontented with things as they are. In other words, culture is not only absorbed; it is also criticized and remade. Organized education hands down the mores and the skills of the group to each succeeding generation of newcomers, not only as something to be accepted and used, but also as something to be reformed. It is a part of the educational process to give the responsive child the tools of criticism and the instruments of that possible reformation.

This second responsibility of education, to help the individual remold the society in which he finds himself, is important for the child; in the continued learning of the adult, it is fundamental. We may say to the child that he comes to school to learn the things that others tell him he must know. He must form his personality in the cultural pattern.[1] The adult already has the pattern. He is living in it. But he wants to change his position in it or he wants to modify the pattern itself. The agency

[1] Cf. Ruth Benedict, *Patterns of Culture*, Houghton Mifflin Company, 1934, Chap. III.

that helps him is thus put to purposes both personal and social but the initiative, in a free society, remains with the individual.

Since we live in a self-governing nation, in which public institutions must be adapted to the needs and desires of the public, it is important to note here that the public itself undergoes modification. Not only do we have a difference due to the slow rise of general educational standards which would naturally lead to a greater interest in further study. Our population also slowly changes in composition, particularly in the general age level. In 1900 the proportion of the total population above the age of twenty was 55.6 per cent. In 1920 the proportion over twenty was 59.2 per cent, and in 1930 it was 61.2 per cent. In 1920 the proportion of children of pre-school age in our total population was 11 per cent. In 1930 this had decreased to 9.3 per cent. In that decade the total number of children under five declined.[1] It is the recorded opinion of most students of demography that the slackening gross birth rate, the lengthening of the average life, and the other factors in our situation are producing a people older and older as time goes on. Adult education becomes a more serious problem when there are more people, proportionately, of adult age. It may even be true in time that we shall find ourselves, in many places, with school equipment built for a child population no longer large enough to make full use of it.

This older population is now faced with acute and distressing problems of economic and social reconstruction. But in thinking of adult education as a social movement, it is well to remember that it is not tied to a social crisis. Many of those most deeply interested mistakenly speak as if it were only an instrument for changing the social

[1] Thompson and Whelpton, *Population Trends in the United States*, McGraw-Hill, 1933, p. 109.

order. No doubt it can be used for this great and necessary purpose. But no society, no matter how perfected, will ever need adult education less. If efforts for social betterment succeed, adult education will be not only as much needed in the future as it is now, it will also be much more sought after. The characteristic of a better society will be the more generous provision of opportunities for self-improvement by a more generally awakened people.

The tendency to speak of adult learning as if it were only one of the instruments for bettering society comes no doubt from a failure to realize that the learning process is necessarily concurrent with the whole span of life because problems of profoundly different nature present themselves to the personality at different stages in its development. The old idea, still too common, was that the personality can be made, very early, into a finished product, which is then sent forth to fight its way like an enclosed unity affected only by changes outside itself. But the personality is not a Leibnitzian monad "without windows," nor a molecule of fixed relationships tossed about by "forces." It is much more like a living plant which is affected by environmental circumstances outside, and by principles of growth within.

It is impossible to teach a college youth of eighteen how to meet all the problems of a middle-aged man of fifty. No one can predict just what his problems are going to be at succeeding points in the development of himself and of his social environment. In the best of environments, he himself will be so different a person at the age of fifty that he is incapable now of anticipating the problems and what he will want to do about them. In the most perfect of societies people will still grow up. However much we may use adult education at present as an effective instrument for changing the social pattern, we cannot limit our purposes only to this or any other crisis. Continuing learning will always be needed by the personality as it grows, and, indeed, growth implies learning. Often haphazardly and with too much pain, men and women have always learned from the changes in their own lives. Many of these adjustments are probably beyond the reach of institutional help, and we do not put too much faith in institutions. Organized agencies and pooled social resources can, however, in some degree, speed and make easier the processes through which our lives must go.

QUESTIONS FOR DISCUSSION

(The questions for discussion are an integral part of this book. They are intended not only to test the student's understanding of the more formal sections of the text, but also to carry his thinking further. They will explore the implications of principles and of the social and educational conditions which the student should be able to interpret in his own terms.)

1. Name as many as you can of the great founders of religions, philosophies, and social movements who have addressed their teachings to adults.

2. To people of what age do you usually apply the term "adult"? Do any of the people of that age whom you know engage in activities which are not called "education" but are primarily educational in their purpose? Why do they spend their time and energy in that way?

3. What would happen in the United States if all schools of all kinds closed their doors and all teachers were put to work at something else?

4. Find in some book on the philosophy of education what you consider a satisfactory definition of education as a social institution (not merely as environmental influence). Apply the definition to the personal problems of a normal man or woman of forty-five years. Criticize it from that standpoint.

READING REFERENCES

BEARD, CHARLES A., "Electric Fire of Thought," *Journal of Adult Education*, Vol. II, No. 1, January, 1930.

CONGDON and HENRY, *Adult Education*, a bibliography with annotations and an introduction, Michigan School Service Company (Lansing), 1934.

FISHER, DOROTHY CANFIELD, *Learn or Perish*, Liveright Publishing Corporation, 1930.

KEPPEL, F. P., *Education for Adults*, Columbia University Press, 1926.

KOTINSKY, RUTH, *Adult Education and the Social Scene*, D. Appleton-Century Co., 1933.

LINDEMAN, E. C., *The Meaning of Adult Education*, New Republic, Inc., 1926.

PROCTOR, WILLIAM MARTIN, *Annotated Bibliography on Adult Education*, Frank Wiggins Trade School (Los Angeles), 1935.

STANLEY, OLIVER H., *The Way Out: Essays on the Meaning and Purpose of Adult Education*, Oxford University Press, 1923.

Chapter Two

THE PAST

MATERIALS are not yet available for writing a complete history of adult education in the United States. But we may usefully examine some elements of the movement up to about the year 1926. Since then it has taken the more definite shape whose elements will be described at some length in this book.

American adult education has not been of a single and systematic character. It has never been a folk movement for the refashioning of a national culture like that undertaken in Denmark under the leadership of Bishop Grundtvig. It has not been largely a movement for the intellectual improvement of the underprivileged, particularly the "working class," as in Great Britain. Nor has it ever been a definite concern of the government, used to propagate a political philosophy as in Italy and Russia, and more recently in Germany. It has always been carried on by a wide variety of agencies, for a variety of purposes, and with many different kinds of people. For this reason, some critics have called it formless and without direction. Actually it has penetrated to more phases of life in America than in any other country. It has been thoroughly in accord with our basic democratic idea that education is a common right, that learning is neither something reserved for an aristocracy nor something bequeathed by a superior class to inferiors.

Most American adult-education enterprises have been
organized voluntarily, even when carried on under
public auspices. They have expressed the complexity and
vitality of American life.

Four institutions, none of them uniquely American
but all indigenous in development and in character,
played a part as historical forerunners. Contemplation
of their history is not altogether reassuring to one who
is deeply concerned for the future, but they all left
traces of good in our attitudes and they all accomplished much in their best periods. These four are lyceums, chautauquas, correspondence schools, and women's
clubs.

LYCEUMS

The first lyceum was organized in Milbury, Massachusetts, in 1826, and within a year at least ten other New
England villages had followed the example. In another
year, there were approximately one hundred branches
of a loosely organized system. Here, as in many other
phases of adult education at various times in the past,
the efforts of one person spread the idea. Josiah Holbrook of Derby, Connecticut, was a tireless and evidently successful public lecturer on the branches of
science which at that time were popular in New England, particularly geology. The lore of the earth and its
rocks attracted people then as astronomy and the play
of stars in the mysterious distant spaces fascinate the
layman now. Not only in New England but throughout
the British Isles there are today dust-covered collections
of stones that bear witness to what was once an intellectual passion. Holbrook lectured and had enough
imagination to see that an interest in science could lead
to an interest in history, in art, or in public questions.

He wanted, according to his own statement, "to improve conversation by introducing worth-while topics into the daily intercourse of families, neighbors, and friends."

His efforts both as practitioner and promoter, and the response of people who saw in the popular lecture course a chance to improve their own intellectual condition had led by 1834 to the establishment of some 3,000 town lyceums extending straight across the country as far as Detroit and generally down into the South. In 1831, a huge meeting was held in New York for the organization of the "National American Lyceum" to which delegates came, representing a thousand towns. This organization lasted for eight years, and widespread interest in local lyceums survived. The lyceums were in full swing up to the Civil War. Four years of bigotry and violence in the 60's did much to break up the habits of peaceful discussion and common thought which they had encouraged.

In its heyday the lyceum was an institution important enough to enlist the talent of Daniel Webster as presiding officer in Boston, and many a name familiar to American school children today was made familiar to their great-grandparents through the popular lectures which were the main professional occupation of men like Emerson, Thoreau, Lowell, Holmes, Hale, Henry Ward Beecher, Wendell Phillips, and many others.

One lesson to be learned from the lyceum at its height is of considerable importance today. Josiah Holbrook listed among the things which he thought lyceums could do, "to increase the advantages and raise the character of existing district schools." These lecture meetings, genuine adult-education enterprises, were a common part of the social life of artisans and storekeepers before public schools were established and, in fact, before public schools were acceptable to most of the taxpayers of this country. There is good reason to believe that the public-

school system of Massachusetts and the pioneering of
Horace Mann got popular support because of things said
and done in lyceum meetings. In other words, the education of parents helped to build better schools for children.

After the Civil War, lecturing and promoting lecturers
became a business. In 1868 several national lecture
bureaus were organized, using the same name as the
more spontaneously created community enterprises.
Commercial methods were applied. Publicity was beginning to be understood and salesmanship was revived
or invented as an art. Lecturers sponsored by promoters
were no longer willing to speak for the "five dollars and
oats for my horse" which once were enough for Emerson.
Celebrity, whether savory or not, began to have a commercial value greater than scholarly competence. The
lecture business of today, with all its good and bad
features, is the result.

Lyceum systems were changing into commercial lecture bureaus, but some educators continued to believe
that lectures could be and should be primarily educational. Even before the revival of the public forum
movement a few years ago, there were notable experiments. Some light might be got from a study of the career
of Henry F. Leipziger and a search, which would be
fruitless, for traces of his work in the city of New York
where he lived.

Most of what is being said today on behalf of adult
learning can be found in the speeches and reports of
Leipziger. He was a heroic personality, an immigrant
Jew, who devoted most of his life to building up the
public-school lecture system. There had been night
schools in New York City for two generations before he
began in 1891, but they offered little more than formal
continuation work. When he took charge of the lectures,
attendance was almost immediately multiplied by three,

although the cost of the lectures to the city remained the same. In the next quarter century, until his death, his own personal enthusiasm and administrative ability pushed the public lecture system of New York into a development which can be summarized for 1914–15 in these figures:

Number of meetings	5,515
Aggregate attendance	1,295,907
Cost to the city	$140,000

He had begun with an appropriation of a tenth of that and a total attendance of one sixtieth. He secured the services of many of the most notable men of his time for small fees. Immediately after his death, interest began to slacken.

There are few incidents in our educational history more worth studying. Two explanations were given in 1928 and have often been given since for the rise and fall of the Leipziger lecture idea. One is that the coming of the radio and the improvement of the moving pictures destroyed the audience. The second is that the loss of Dr. Leipziger's own dynamic management made the scheme unworkable. There may, of course, be some truth in both of these explanations. But it should not be overlooked that when the lectures were finally closed out, thousands of people protested bitterly that something was being taken from them for which they had no substitute. Still more important is it to remember that Dr. Leipziger had to fight for every appropriation he ever received, in spite of the impressive record. He left an institution and a following, but official minds were not convinced.

CHAUTAUQUAS

Similar to the lyceums, but coming a little later, were the "chautauquas." The word "chautauqua" has in

American social history two quite distinct meanings, and many people are unaware of the difference. The "Chautauqua Institution" has had a fine record in genuine adult education. But many people, on hearing the word, think of second-rate entertainment or oratory. The Chautauqua Institution was founded in 1871, on the shores of the lake of the same name in western New York, as a summer training camp for Sunday-school teachers in the Methodist Church. The founders were Bishop J. H. Vincent and Lewis Miller. The present typical summer season at Chautauqua, which Theodore Roosevelt called the most peculiarly American thing to be seen in America, includes successfully many types of adult education: music, art, drama, current problems, and study groups. Many of the visitors to the beautiful little fenced-in town by the lake still devote a large part of their time to religious problems, to the discussion of missionary campaigns and other church matters. The talks given in the open-air amphitheater are by the same notable lecturers one hears talking and being questioned by critical audiences elsewhere. The symphony orchestra is of first-rate quality. The opera house prides itself on its production of the new as well as the old masterpieces. The theater school, the arts and crafts school, the library school, and all the other branches make a people's vacation university. By means of reading circles and a recommended list of books the influence of the Chautauqua by the lake has been spread to every corner of the country.

The name "chautauqua" was taken over by commercial circuits of tent shows when the fame of the original institution spread. The traveling companies, which went mostly into smaller towns, included orators, musicians, actors, and "entertainers." The performers were of all kinds, good, bad, indifferent. Not many of their programs could be fairly judged by the standards

of the original Chautauqua. By less rigorous standards,
they doubtless served an educational purpose in their
time. When communication of ideas was without either
the advantages or the dangers of cinema and radio,
many a village dweller felt in the summer's show a
breath of the outside world. He came, perhaps, to be
amused by the bell ringers but stayed to think, stirred by
the speech of a young politician or an old preacher. Now,
however, the tent shows are mostly gone. They left a
quaint reputation against which the summer school by
Lake Chautauqua has to struggle. It preceded them and
has outlasted them, and continues to count in the movement of today.

WOMEN'S CLUBS

The women's clubs were pioneers also and are, in
many ways, the most remarkable of all the agencies by
which American people have undertaken to educate
themselves. Dorothy Canfield Fisher finds their origin in
the change of manners after the Civil War which made
good health and energy fashionable for women, and in
the sociological changes which moved industry out of
the home and robbed housekeepers of most of their economic functions. These causes, working together perhaps
with the constantly rising educational level of the whole
people, gave women the courage to form their own self-
improvement societies. In spite of ridicule and masculine
opposition, women's clubs from the 70's to the present
have been educational institutions of genuine value.

Here also there has been some attempt at commercial-
ization, but clubs formed for the special purpose of buy-
ing expensive sets of books have never amounted to much
in comparison with the tremendous spread of indigenous
and self-controlled clubs of ambitious women.

There are signs today that the historic function of the women's club has been in some degree fulfilled. In rural areas and in smaller towns the club with a widely diverse program and amateur guidance is still healthy and bids fair to persist for a long time. In the larger urban centers, the general program organization seems to be failing to renew its memberships from among the daughters of its present members. This probably is not because of less interest in club activity. It is rather because the younger women are being drawn into associations with more specific interests. The League of Women Voters, the American Association of University Women, the Business and Professional Women's Clubs, the Junior League, and a wide variety of other societies carry on. What has happened is not so much the decline of the movement as its change into more specialized forms because of the fact that more women are in the professions and more have received college training. This change confirms the importance of the historic role that clubs have played in the past.

CORRESPONDENCE SCHOOLS

Instruction by letters is a very old form of teaching. It had been used in formal education in Europe for at least a generation before the formation in America, in 1873, of the Society to Encourage Studies at Home. The so-called Correspondence University at Ithaca, New York, in 1883, the extension of correspondence from the Chautauqua Institution, and several other attempts to teach academic subjects, particularly languages, by means of letters all came at about the same time. The work of William Rainey Harper at Chautauqua grew into the correspondence work of the extension division in

the University of Chicago when Dr. Harper became its
president.

There are two clearly distinguishable lines of development, the private or commercial ventures and the teaching by mail, or "home-study" work, of college extension
departments. College extension will be discussed later.[1]
Our interest here is in the pioneering efforts of the private
schools. Lengthy consideration of such schools is outside
our scope since they are primarily business enterprises.
But in any description of the threads of the past that
have been woven into the web of modern opportunities,
due credit must be given to their long campaigns to
arouse men and women to a realization of the advantages of continuing learning.

The commercial correspondence school of today is
traced to the experiment of a Pennsylvania citizen.
Thomas A. Foster, editor of the *Mining Herald* of Shen-
andoah, Pennsylvania, began in the 80's to publish questions and answers dealing with the problems of safety
in the mines. This was expanded later into a regular
course by which miners could study the various phases
of their own jobs as well as the safety methods in which
Foster was originally interested. Out of this grew the In-
ternational Correspondence Schools of Scranton, Pennsylvania, the largest of all the private enterprises.

More than three hundred other private correspondence
schools have sprung up since. Of these, only fifty were,
in 1935, of sufficient scholastic respectability to be members of the National Home Study Council. The Council
was organized in 1926. It inspects private schools in this
field and approves them if they maintain reasonably
high standards. It works toward the elimination of the
unworthy agencies and maintains an information bureau
where students can obtain help in finding desired courses

[1] Cf. Chap. XIII.

in both public and private schools. The agencies outside
the Council's membership range from the Council's high
standard down to blatant charlatanism. Regulating commercial correspondence schools is difficult. Few states
have statutes to protect the unwary student against
swindling, and a school set up in any state can operate in
any other as long as] it does not come under the fraud
regulations of the postal department.

Commercial correspondence study is handicapped by
having to make very definite economic promises to its
students. And some of the schools are accused of caring only to get students enrolled, without any concern
thereafter that they should finish the courses. Some of
them spend the larger part of their great revenues for
advertising and salesmanship rather than for instruction.

There are at the present time, however, more people
enrolled in commercial correspondence courses than
there are in all the higher educational institutions of
America. And it is necessary to consider, as will be done
in the chapter on Special Methods what possibilities
there are in correspondence for the adults who have no
access to any direct form of instruction. Whatever balance
may be struck between good and bad in the present development, the commercial home-study agencies of the
nineteenth century helped to build up the general popular interest in adult learning.

"AMERICANIZATION"

The World War brought another activity into the
picture. Public schools had been for some time engaged,
not very actively, in the cure of illiteracy. And they had
for generations been carrying on continuation schools
and some types of occupational training for young adults

which were known as adult education but were scarcely
of the same broad character as what has developed since.
During the excitement of wartime and in the spirit of
nationalism then dominant, the schools were made the
instrument of an impulse to "Americanize" the large
immigrant sections of our people.

The millions of immigrants in this country, many of
whom were segregated in ingrowing cultural groups, had
not been a public concern to any extent and their in-
duction into American ways had been carried on mostly
by their own societies. Almost overnight they became a
public responsibility because they appeared to be a
public danger. Haphazard legislation, using the public
schools, attempted to cure in a few months the mistakes
of generations. Private societies put pressure upon the
schools to hurry up the Americanizing of somewhat be-
wildered men and women. This hysteria, luckily, did
not much affect the teachers. Solid adult education was
achieved on the impetus of this new interest in a special
group. The study of the English language and of the
American constitution was the chief occupation of the
classes.

Since the close of the war, two changes in the situation
have led to a sharp decline in "Americanization." In the
first place, the number of aliens entering the country has
been cut down to almost none. In the second place, the
emotional nationalism of wartime has faded and good
sense has restored the realization that immigrants brought
culture with them that was of great value to America.
Sympathy, instead of pressure, has guided more of the
efforts to induct these voluntary citizens into their place
in American society. They are being encouraged not
only to take on the new folkways of their new home but
also to keep alive and hand on the folk art they brought
with them. Typical of twenty years ago was a group of

reluctant "foreigners" being lectured at by a salesman of American ideals. Typical of the present is a folk festival in which the children of all nations are given a chance to re-create the cultural values of their homelands.

Tangible values for adult education were produced by this over-zealous movement. Much of the aesthetic content of the program in many centers comes directly out of the Americanization process in its new forms. Secondly, a group of professional teachers concerned with the problems of the adult, later organized as the Department of Adult Education of the National Education Association, have carried over into the broader program their interest and the skills which they acquired in a time of trouble. There are doubtless still large sections of the public which think of this highly important work as the whole of adult education. States which have separate divisions in their state education department, for this kind of work, and many cities which have active night high schools owe their established agencies to wartime anxiety.

HISTORY

Sometime in the future a history of adult education in America will be written. It will sum up the contributions of the agencies which have been mentioned and of many others. Only then will it be possible to measure the strength of each impulse and the result of each attempt, abortive or carried through. Any history written will probably take the year 1926, or thereabouts, as a turning point. At that time, the movement ceased to be a combination of sporadic and scattered impulses, public and private both, some of which were doing noteworthy work, and began to take shape as an organization of community resources for community betterment. It is not likely that any really new ideas have been invented since 1926. Workers have been drawn together not by new arguments but because of the rapid industrial and social changes which have detached millions of grown men and women from their cultural moorings and made them anxious to find their way among new ideas.

Three events contributed largely to the developments of the last decade. First, teachers and administrators in the public schools of America began to feel a greater response to the widening intellectual demands of the adult population and to see greater opportunities for usefulness. Second, agricultural extension was widely established. Third, the American Association for Adult Education began its career as the most influential agency for determining general purposes and philosophy and as the greatest stimulus to experimentation through the use of funds granted by the Carnegie Corporation. These three major influences were institutional, and they will all be discussed later. Listing them is not intended to shut out from recognition a number of teachers and leaders who, from various points of vantage, developed and expressed fruitful ideas.

The study of the past, when it can be thoroughly carried out, will be useful because it will show how solid are the impulses upon which the movement is based, and how successfully workers have met various problems in different times and places. It will also help the workers in public and private institutions and the individuals who have been pursuing their own careers in raising the level of public intellectual activity to see their relationship to a wider movement and their proper place in a gradual development. It will help to quiet the fears of the uninformed who even now look upon adult education as an attempt to make up for the mistakes of the ordinary schooling of our children. Adult education can then be understood as a social movement, arising naturally out of native impulses and satisfying a permanent and growing need.

<h2 align="center">QUESTIONS FOR DISCUSSION</h2>

1. Do you know of any modern instances in which the self-education interests of parents have led them to give more intelligent and active support to the community's system for educating their children? Why is this likely to happen?

2. Contrast the club activities of women with the club activities of men in your own community. Have the programs of either group materially changed during the time of your observation?

3. If you have ever subscribed to a lecture course, what motives led you to do so? How do you think your own reasons compared with those of the other members of the audience? Did you get what you wanted out of the course? If not, why not?

4. What national reasons can you give for a program of "Americanization?" What social reasons? What arguments can you give for preserving alien cultures in American life?

5. What new social devices and habits do you think have contributed to the decline of the "tent chautauquas"?

<h2 align="center">READING REFERENCES</h2>

ALDERMAN, L. R., "Adult Education 1928–1930," *U. S. Office of Education Biennial Survey of Education 1928–1930*, I, pp. 419–41.

BOJE, ANDREAS, *Education in Denmark*, Oxford University Press, 1932.

CARTWRIGHT, MORSE A., *Ten Years of Adult Education*, The Macmillan Company, 1935.

FISHER, DOROTHY CANFIELD, *Why Stop Learning?* Harcourt, Brace and Company, 1927.

FRANKEL, RUTH L., *Henry M. Leipziger*, The Macmillan Company, 1933.

HURLBURT, J. L., *The Story of Chautauqua*, G. P. Putnam's Sons, 1921.

MAGNUS, PHILIP, "Adult Education in Ancient Times," *Edinburgh Review*, Vol. CCXXXVII, p. 78.

NOFFSINGER, J. S., *Correspondence Schools, Lyceums, Chautauquas*, The Macmillan Company, 1926.

PEFFER, NATHANIEL, *New Schools for Older Students*, The Macmillan Company, 1926.

TALBOT AND ROSENBERRY, *The History of the American Association of University Women*, Houghton Mifflin Company, 1931.

Chapter Three

FUNCTIONS OF ADULT EDUCATION

AN EDUCATIONAL activity can be considered in terms of
function, of agency, or of subject matter. One can try to
understand it by what it tries to do, or by the institutions
which carry on the programs, or by the content of its
teaching. It can be approached in still other ways, of
course, such as by describing its clientele, and that we
have already done in some measure for adult education.
Very little will be said in this brief book about subject
matter; most of the principles and methods we shall discuss apply to nearly all subjects. Functions and agencies
are our direct concern. We will analyze the first in order
to understand what adult education tries to do, and look
at some of the agencies later in order to see it in operation.

If we are to attempt an analysis of functional aims, it
will be necessary to keep in mind the rapidly changing
character of the movement. No attempt will be made to
fix this changing character. We shall only say, tentatively,
that adult education may be divided, according to function, into five types. An agency may engage in any one
or in all of these five types, and a particular activity may
cover more than one of the five purposes. Fundamentally,
they are all the same purpose, the enlargement of the
personality and the quickening of life. The deeper we go
into the motives of mature men and women who are

setting out to educate themselves, the more we are convinced that this fundamental motive, self-improvement,
expresses itself in a thousand different ways but remains
always the same.

The five functions of adult education are: Remedial,
Occupational, Relational, Liberal, and Political.

Remedial adult training is more or less formal study
undertaken to give a person of adult years whatever he
needs to bring his educational equipment up to the
minimum that is necessary for life in an American community. It includes the ability to read and to write, and
for immigrants it includes also a knowledge of spoken
English and of American citizenship. Training in homemaking and child care on an elementary basis, in all the
simple rules of health and civilized behavior, are also
remedial since grown citizens are presumed to have a
working minimum.

Occupational training may be: (*a*) for advancement
on the job; (*b*) for advancement to another job of a
different sort; (*c*) for the industrial rehabilitation of the
victim of machine unemployment; (*d*) for guidance in
choosing or adjusting to an occupation.

Relational education includes "parent education" and
also the studies of emotions, attitudes, and psychological
habits which are designed to help us better to understand
ourselves and our relations with other persons.

"Liberal education" is the best term available to describe activities which are undertaken chiefly for their own
sake, for the pleasure that is in them. Although all adult
studies should be liberal and "liberating," the first two
types listed above are instrumental, and to a lesser extent the third also. They are expected to produce results
beyond the satisfaction of achievement. In the pursuit of
art, or philosophy, or science, one could find, no doubt,
the motive of self-advancement, but these activities are

not so directly applicable to one's daily life or to one's daily human relations. And the recreational element, the sheer enjoyment of pleasant effort, although it also is, or should be, present in every form of educational activity, is stronger perhaps in this field than elsewhere.

Political education includes all those studies, practices, and experiences which men deliberately undertake to make themselves better members of the commonwealth. This includes not only the study of "politics" as a subject, but also all forms of training for political action.

As all adult effort at learning is derived in some degree out of the desire for the improvement of one's own personality, and as it should all have recreational value, so likewise all this activity, whether formal or informal, scholastic or non-scholastic, whether pursued in solitary devotion or under the guidance of an inspired leader should always have as a further purpose an increase in the student's own power of self-direction. The social element need not and doubtless will not ever go out entirely from adult education. Learning together is one of the joys and one of the advantages of self-education. But a constant growth in independent thinking power and in the capacity for the management of one's own program is an essential aim, implicit in all other purposes.

THE REMEDIAL FUNCTION

Remedial education should be, as time goes on, less and less a burden upon our resources, but it is not likely ever to be completely unnecessary. We can, if we are ever willing to devote enough time and money to the purpose, completely eradicate illiteracy from the American people. If simple literacy is attained, however, a higher standard will by that time be commonly accepted, and the lower fringes of our population, educationally speaking—the men and women who will have failed to get a fair share of educational opportunities in their youth—will still be noticeably below the constantly advancing average.

Most Americans have a much too cheerful picture of the educational accomplishments of their own people. This is due perhaps to the fact that education is most talked about where it is most carried on. Education is a common topic of conversation and a common matter of concern to all forward-looking people in those communities where it has accomplished enough to make its purposes well known and where, also, it is exemplified in well-managed school systems and ostentatious school buildings. There are wide regions of America, less often thought of, where education is so backward that the lack of it is scarcely felt. These regions are social as well as geographical; that is, they exist in sections of our large cities where life is intellectually remote from the current of American culture as well as in regions like the hill country of the eastern seaboard, parts of the deep south, and parts of the southwest, where backwardness is general.

Few people, aside from those who have made special studies of this problem, are aware of its extent. We think of ourselves generally as a literate people, but the word "literate" is capable of many interpretations. Those who have spent most time investigating the facts behind the census records are agreed that there are millions of grown men and women in America who are still not literate by any real standard. They may be capable of signing their own names if necessary, but they cannot use written or printed speech as an instrument for business or for learning. It is considered a conservative estimate that there are fifteen million men and women in America above the age of twenty years who are thus handicapped.

Fifteen million people comprise 20 per cent of America's adult citizens. These people cannot fairly be said to possess the instruments of political and social knowledge with which to play their parts in a free, self-governing country. In spite of these facts, the cure of illiteracy is sometimes dismissed as of no present importance. It is said that we need only to repair our school system sufficiently so that no one can in the future grow up without having learned the minimum requirements of active citizenship.

This solution is not acceptable for two reasons. In the first place, it is very difficult to find support for good schools in a region where good schooling is not understood by parents. A genuine intellectual quickening, if it is effective in any community, must penetrate all ages and all classes. It may be thought that there is very little gained by teaching an old person to read or to write since, with few years left to run, he is not likely to make use of his new-found skill. This, of course, is ignoring the human value of happiness in achievement which by any gracious and generous standard must mean as much to an old person as to the young. But worse, it ignores also the fact that in communities where illiteracy is common there is a primitive respect for age, which makes it exceedingly important that the very old be interested in anything which is to become, so to speak, fashionable for everybody. At an educational conference, a worker from the South spoke of the triumphant acquirement of literacy by a man ninety years old. A skeptic inquired what good there was in giving such an aged person a skill which he could never live to use. The answer was that the old man had nearly a hundred descendants. When Grandpappy learned to read, all the rest of them acknowledged that it might be a good thing for them to do. In this incident is much truth concerning the conditions and the social motivation of those communities where illiteracy is common among all classes and where it is most difficult to find reasons which will appeal to the average person and lead him to try to cure his backwardness.

The second reason for giving remedial education a secure place in planning has already been indicated. Our "minimum" standard is not fixed. It rises constantly, and until we have fully equal opportunities for all our youth, if indeed we can ever hope to accomplish that, we can do the next best thing, which is to remedy the damage that early inequalities have caused.

A common minimum standard of education, however, includes more than the ability to read and write. There are elements of homemaking, of the care of children, of health, and of citizenship in general, which call for very much the same sort of treatment. Then there are large numbers of people in America who are debarred from citizenship because they lack sufficient knowledge of our laws and customs and because they lack knowledge of the English language, however well educated they may be in one or more foreign tongues. These people also fall within the ranks of "remedial" learners, and special methods are needed for solving their problems.

It is possible to carry on education of the kinds here mentioned in a utilitarian fashion which might perhaps suffice for the immediate object. But that would be missing an opportunity of tremendous social importance. Here again, one's approach to the problem of the illiterate and underprivileged depends very largely upon his social philosophy. If it is presumed without evidence that those who are in the underprivileged class have been shaken down into that lower position because of their own lack of native capacity, then these remedial measures will be pursued in no more than a remedial way. They will be no more than the protection which society sets up against the disasters that might come from ignorance and intellectual delinquency among its weaker members. To be sure, such activities can be justified on this ground alone.

On the other hand, a teacher's social philosophy may be of the sort discussed in Chapter Fifteen. He may believe that environments are scarcely ever so favorable as to bring out the best of everybody's powers, and that people of the underprivileged classes may be what they are through no fault of their own. In that case, even remedial work will be thought of as the first step in a process which may well lead to indefinite development of human powers and to the acquisition of great riches for society as a whole.

Whatever the scientific truth may be in regard to the varying capacities of men, there can be no doubt that if a teacher uses a class in beginning English for adults as the means of opening a door into all of civilization's store of learning, which these underprivileged persons may have in the future the chance to acquire, he is devoting his powers to a better purpose. The underprivileged may be those who have had to wait outside the gate, but they need not be forbidden ever to enter. The work of a teacher who can see this opportunity for himself and his pupils changes remedial training into education.

THE OCCUPATIONAL FUNCTION

In discussing further the occupational purposes of adult education, we are still within the range of established public-school activity. There has always been a

greater enthusiasm on the part of administrators and
school boards, as well as a greater sympathy from taxpayers, for occupational training than for most other
phases of an adult-education program. However much
one might criticize this as a crass and limited concept of
public responsibility for the teaching of adults, it should
also be said that occupational training can be made
education in the broadest sense. A motive which is
strictly pragmatic and derived from one's needs on the
job is as good a motive for leading an adult back to
educational experience as any other. If occupational
training is narrow, if it does not lead on, under guidance,
to training which applies to the whole range of an individual's possibilities, that is the fault of the teacher, not
of the subject studied. More will necessarily be said upon
this point under the heading of Method. And more also
must be said in regard to the financing of occupational
training when the general question of public financial
responsibility is taken up later.

It would be theoretically justifiable to consider under
the heading of occupational education all the activities of
professional societies of physicians, lawyers, bankers, and
others, which provide apprenticeship training for their
junior members and advanced study for practitioners.
These are as much adult education as anything, and
they are of very ancient standing. They do not appear to
require any special consideration here, however, since
in the first place they have well-established ways of accomplishing their purposes, innocent for the most part of
any formal method, and since they do not ask either
public interest or public support.

What we are more concerned with here is industrial or
job training. The training needs of the younger adults
are probably well taken care of in most advanced school
systems by continuation schools, by apprenticeship, and

by courses set up under the Smith-Hughes Act. These
are of primary importance. But although they are in one
sense adult education, they are largely a continuation of
secondary-school experience. Great activity in this regard should not be mistaken for genuine interest in the
problem of the older adults.

The typical students in the occupational schools for
older students are those who wish by added labor in their
free time to equip themselves for advancement or for
some more difficult job, and those who are unemployed
because the only thing they can do can be done better
by a machine.

If some of the economists who have dared to make
predictions can be believed, we shall have for some time
in the future, no matter how we may reform our socio-
economic order, a large "pool" of unemployed people.
Men and women will be pushed into this pool by machine
inventions. If all things are properly adjusted, they will
in time climb out again, but the pool will always be
large and the chances for any individual to climb out
and get back into the industrial system will depend almost entirely upon the opportunities given him for acquiring a new skill. If it were not for what we know of
the ability of mature people to gain new aptitudes, this
problem of technological unemployment would be beyond solution, and the human loss from such a situation
would be greater even than the economic. The damage
to self-respect that comes from being reduced to useless-
ness is very difficult to repair. Even more important than
industrial recovery is the restoration of morale to the
victim of industrial collapse.

Here is a task to which the public-education authori-
ties of the future may well direct a share of their human
and financial resources. We may look forward to a time
when a man or woman who has lost a job because a

machine has been found to do his work more cheaply—
because his labor has been "saved"—will turn quite
cheerfully to industrial rehabilitation through public
adult education.

It is well established that the best time for learning
anything is just before one uses it. Education for human
relationships, although necessary in all stages of growth,
cannot be given to a child in such a way as to prepare
him for all the crises of his developing emotional life.
Our concern with the relations of human beings in the
field of adult education has centered largely upon parents
and children. Few things can be taught a child about his
future role as a parent. Most of the problems to which he
will want answers cannot even be explained to him until
after he has found the problems themselves in his own
experience, in his attempts at satisfactory adjustment.

The parent-education movement, widely developed
and a splendid achievement for the most part, has not
been formalized in classroom work. It has depended
heavily upon public-school support, however, and still
more upon the Parent-Teacher Association movement so
closely allied with the public schools. It has developed
an army of specialists and an army of lay leaders. It has
been largely a "folk" movement, an attempt by mothers
to bring the rapidly accumulating scientific knowledge
which means so much in the care and protection of
children into use in their own homes.

Some students of this form of adult education are convinced that too many mistakes are made by amateur
teachers. They believe that the intricate and subtle facts
of psychological relationships should not be discussed by

those who have not had professional training. Against this view, it is urged that there are not, and never can be, enough trained leaders to meet all of the urgent demands for help in child care and in parental adjustment. This opinion suggests that the alternative is not between trained and lay leadership but between lay leadership and leaderless ignorance. And they believe that even a partly equipped leader, particularly if gifted with common sense, willingness to learn, and freedom from dogma, may be useful in friendly discussions of the homely emotional problems of the ordinary family.

This function of adult education includes more, however, than what is usually known as parent education. There are more or less formal ways of studying how to better one's adjustment in all the personal contacts of life which fall necessarily under this designation. And it is important for educators of adults to note that custom is no longer a satisfactory answer to questions of this sort. Sociologists can tell us that through long millenniums of human progress we have solved all such problems by our "folkways." We have done what our fathers and mothers did, even when we did not like the results, because it was sacrilegious or dangerous to do anything else. Our folkways depended upon our tradition and upon authority.

It is needless to point out that this dependence on the authority of custom no longer controls even our closest and most emotionally charged relationships. Whatever one may think about the so-called "experimental" attitude toward life, whatever his philosophy of manners and morals may be, he is compelled to realize that questions of personal relationship can no longer be solved simply by appeal to tradition. We seem to be embarked upon an era of attempted rationality and scientific self-consciousness in these matters. It is an adventure which has its danger and its possibilities. Those who are working in adult education cannot escape becoming involved in it. Here, as elsewhere, resources and methods of adult education must be put at the service of those who would set out rationally to improve themselves.

There is a special responsibility in this field because it is a happy hunting ground for every type of charlatan. The very word "psychology" means to many people, innocent of college courses in the science itself, not a careful discipline of investigation and slow hypothesis, but a romantic kind of magic. The educator of adults enters this field at his peril, but he is compelled to enter since he has to be the guide who points the way from quackery to facts, from fallacies to the humdrum, useful conclusions of science. And by "adult educator" one means to include those thousands of lay leaders already active in the parent-education movement who have struggled tirelessly to do this sometimes thankless work.

THE LIBERAL FUNCTION

All forms of adult education should be in some sense recreational: they should restore confidence, quicken minds, and lead to health, both mental and physical. And all things studied or done should be enjoyable for their own sake. A special division can be made, however, of those things which are liberal, that is, done explicitly because they are enjoyed, and not because they are instrumental to some other purpose. One can divide liberal adult education into the intellectual and the physical, into study and play, not, of course, to suggest that there are no play elements in study and certainly not to say that there are no intellectual elements in physical recreation.

There was a time, not very far back in history, when the kind of education that was called "liberal" was reserved for young men (not for young women) who were destined to positions of importance in governmental or professional affairs. Their liberal education was not intended to fit them for a life of very arduous toil but to refine their minds and manners for leadership in society, a responsibility to which they were entitled by birth and privilege rather than by ability. In the United States, this idea of a liberal education has been generally confined to the eastern seaboard and the older universities, but traces of it are found in all the colleges. And it persists.

With the creation of a new "leisure class," and a general acceptance of the idea that all citizens are equally entitled to what education they can make use of, the ancient notion of a liberal education is no longer of importance. Departing with it will go also most of the older monastic ideas of college life. The college as a place remote from the world, in which young people lived lives shot through with romantic nonsense and terrific intellectual ardors, and out of which they finally came with a hallmark of culture, but putting forever behind them all thoughts of intellectual activity for its own sake —this idea has ceased to have any meaning in American life. If there is to be such a thing as a liberal education in the future, it will be very different, not only because there is a new leisure class demanding these "liberal" advantages, but also because our ideas of education are undergoing rapid changes.

It is not our province here to solve such old riddles as "What studies have educative value, apart from their direct application to training for a particular activity?" That hoary problem we may leave to the psychologists and philosophers of education. We have more to do with such problems as the character of this new leisure class, the function of recreation, and the usefulness and availability of liberal studies in the civic development of America.

Is the new leisure class prepared for its new opportunity? It is made up of working people whose hours of necessary labor are being rapidly shortened. The doubt as to their wise use of free time reflects somewhat the eighteenth-century morality, which thought it was best for little children to slave in the factories because otherwise they might fall into evil habits. Have leisure classes of the past been wise in the use of their freedom? For the most part, the people in history who have not been compelled to labor for their bread have spent their time in idleness, debauchery, violence, wars, or aimlessness. This does not mean that all the people to whom leisure was given have wasted their time; we know that out of classes securely placed in the economic order have come many of our ablest men and women, devoted to public service. The leisure class itself has a curious record in Western history because for the most part its members have been largely useless, insofar as they enjoyed their leisure at all; but many of our greatest achievements have been the work either of those who were born to that class or of those who enjoyed the favor of some member of the leisure class and thus were enabled to escape the hard necessities of labor and devote themselves to the arts, to literature, to science, to philosophy, or to whatever it was they were gifted to produce. Be that as it may, a great number of men and women whose lives of toil have been materially shortened within recent decades and whose free time may be still further extended are probably as well able to use their time wisely as were the leisure classes of the past.

This, however, does not quite settle the question. The

creation and sustaining appreciation of cultural values have come largely out of the free-time activities of those who enjoyed occasional freedom. It is idle to speculate as to the possible creativeness of the new free time of working men and women. The question for us is the educational one. Is there any responsibility for making their new-found liberty more rewarding to those who enjoy it? Who bears this responsibility?

One can examine this question fairly without in any sense assuming that educators or others have a right to say to any group of people that they must spend their leisure in any way but what they chose for themselves. They have the same right to experiment as other classes have had. They are free to choose. But society cannot discharge its obligation to the new leisure class by any simple doctrine of *laissez faire*. Society as a whole, and particularly education as an institution, can enlarge the range of choices open to these who have new freedom.

Freedom itself is partly a matter of knowledge; one cannot choose to do something he has never heard of. It is folly to say that a man does not enjoy good music if he has never heard any. Neither the man himself, nor those who undertake to interpret his desires, can say what he will choose among the treasures of the world's culture until he has been sufficiently exposed to them to have at least some slight acquaintance. Consequently, there is a direct responsibility to see that all the finest things are made easily accessible to those who may now come to enjoy them.

Patience is necessary. The formation of taste is a process, not an act of miraculous grace. And it is a process in which we can have considerable confidence. By this time we have had enough experience with the radio, the phonograph, inexpensive reprints of good pictures, amateur drama, and dozens of other experiments in spreading the finer forms of recreation and pleasure. We know that things which are essentially better will hold their own against the cheap and trivial and in the end will win the loyalty of a constantly enlarging circle. Consequently, the provision of adult education in the "liberal" studies and in the arts is mostly a matter of providing opportunities. Teaching in this field cannot be forced. Recent investigations, particularly in the field of music, indicate, however, that more help in leisure-time activities would be asked for if the seekers could be sure that help would be sympathetically and intelligibly given.

Liberal education is more than a matter of recreation even in the highest of aesthetic pursuits. We are using the term here to cover all those activities carried on for their own sake. And surely among them we must include such studies as science, philosophy, history, and literature. We may not have so many young people in our "liberal" colleges in the future. But whether this happens or not, the demand for these pleasures and these profitable ways of spending free time is certain to increase far beyond the capacity of organized institutional study. A more general demand for liberal education is certain, and nothing but the resources of the adult-education movement can possibly meet it. Colleges may be devoted to highly professionalized study and training. The liberalizing education which will become more and more a matter of course for every citizen will be left mostly to the free-time activities of later years.

THE POLITICAL FUNCTION

The phases of adult education already discussed are in some senses political; they are all conducive to better citizenship. But direct political education is necessary. Here, as in no other field, we find daily exemplified the truth of the psychological principle that things should be learned immediately before they are used. Heroic efforts on the part of secondary-school teachers have thus far accomplished comparatively little in improving the politics of the average American town. This may be due to the fact that we have not as yet succeeded in getting a sufficient proportion of our population through the secondary schools. The percentage of our general adult citizenry which has been through a secondary school is still small. But secondary-school training for citizenship, no matter how wisely carried out, still faces probable failure unless support is brought to it in the adult experiences of those whose political education it begins.

In the first place, as the child grows up, he finds that public questions have a very different character when he begins to discuss them as a responsible citizen. And he also finds, no matter how realistic a teacher has tried to be, that the world of affairs cannot be actively reflected in the classroom. If he has achieved a degree of tolerance and open-mindedness, a certain political honesty, and a certain skepticism toward reckless propaganda, much has already been achieved. But these are only the materials out of which his citizenship can be constructed in the actual experience of adult life. In this difficult task he needs accurate, trustworthy information. When provided with information, he needs also—and this is the greatest lack at present in American life— the chance to talk over public business with his fellow citizens.

All institutions and groups that have political purposes claim to be educational. This is not the place to speak again of the vexed question as to whether or not all educational activity should be based upon a definite doctrine and should try to make converts. If our present concern with adult education as a phase of our general social system yields any new knowledge as to techniques of learning, or persuasion, or enlightenment, these techniques will be and should be at the disposal of all partisan groups. We can for the moment, however, distinguish adult education as such from the institutions that carry on propaganda for partisan purposes. In the political realm, educational activities are, first, providing for discussion of public questions; and second, adapting public documents and technical writings to help the ordinary citizen to understand his country's business.

Very little need be said about the necessity for these two activities. Questions of method will be postponed to another section of this book. The statement is often made that political adult education is an attempt "to make democracy work." [1] The complication and formidable quantity of public business have made it very difficult for the average man, even with the best intentions, to keep up with public affairs. It is doubtless an illusion to suppose that he can ever understand thoroughly the public problems that baffle experts. But he cannot escape his moral responsibility for choosing competent and honest representatives, nor can he escape the major decisions. He cannot expect his representatives, no matter how capable or conscientious, to do their business best except in an atmosphere of understanding and a widespread knowledge of the public problems involved. Hence, without expecting to make of every man an expert in all of the technical and practical aspects of every public matter, we may still say that active discussion of public business is a necessity in a democracy. Discussion can be practiced in public forums. The next step, the preparation of trustworthy materials which will bring

[1] John W. Studebaker, *The American Way*, McGraw-Hill Book Company, 1935, Chap. II.

information about public questions within the range of the reading habits and capacities of the average man, has not yet been successfully managed. Experiments are now under way, and a general interest in this type of material will in time produce results.

These five kinds of education are the functions of the movement at the present time: Remedial, Occupational, Relational, Liberal, and Political. In all of them there is the further purpose of increasing constantly the student's powers of self-development and self-direction.

QUESTIONS FOR DISCUSSION

1. How would you classify the functions of secondary education? Of college education? Of graduate work in a university?

2. Compare the motives of a college undergraduate studying history with those of a women's club member following a reading course in the same subject.

3. Are any of the five functions analyzed in the text incompatible with any of the others; that is, are there any two of them which could not be served by an agency at the same time with the same student or students?

4. How does success in the remedial function contribute toward success in the political?

5. Which of the five functions do you consider of most importance at the present time? What likely changes in social conditions would rearrange this order of importance? How?

READING REFERENCES

BURNS, C. DELISLE, *Leisure in the Modern World*, D. Appleton-Century Co., 1932.

CARTWRIGHT, MORSE A., ed., *Unemployment and Adult Education*, American Association for Adult Education, 1931.

COOK AND WALKER, *Adult Elementary Education*, Charles Scribner's Sons, 1927.

EVANS, O. D., *Educational Opportunities for Young Workers*, The Macmillan Company, 1926.

GRUENBERG, SIDONIE M., ed., *Report of Sub-Committee on Types of Parent Education* (White House Conference on Child Health and Protection), D. Appleton-Century Co., 1932.

JACKS, L. P., *Education through Recreation*, Harper and Brothers, 1932.

LEE, E. A., ed., *Objectives and Problems of Vocational Education*, McGraw-Hill Book Company, 1928.

NEILSON, W. A., ed., *Roads to Knowledge*, W. W. Norton and Company, 1932.

OVERSTREET, HARRY A., *A Guide to Civilized Leisure*, W. W. Norton and Company, 1934.

OVERSTREET, HARRY A., *Influencing Human Behavior*, W. W. Norton and Company, 1925.

PEFFER, NATHANIEL, *Educational Experiments in Industry*, The Macmillan Company, 1932.

STUDEBAKER, JOHN W., *The American Way*, McGraw-Hill Book Company, 1935.

Chapter Four

HOW ADULTS LEARN

EVEN AS recently as William James, psychologists have believed that men could learn very little after they had attained physical maturity. James asserted that few men got any new ideas after the age of 25. And most of the old saws ran to the effect that the mind of a child was plastic and the mind of the adult fixed and immovable. Sporadic experiments have gone on for a long time in the hope of getting light on this extremely important matter, but not until Edward L. Thorndike, Professor of Psychology in Teachers College, Columbia University, published his work, *Adult Learning*, in 1928 was anything really definite known. This does not mean that other experimenters had not begun to accumulate the kind of data which Thorndike and his associates systematically assembled and studied. But the catalytic effect of Thorndike's work upon the scattered thinking that was going on justifies one in saying that a genuine belief in the power of adults to learn effectively was established by his publication.

It is worth noting in passing, however, that our common view of the power of adults to learn was contrary to our practice. A child spends a very large share of his earlier years in acquiring the vocabulary, pronunciation, and grammar of his native language, and all his experiences contribute largely to this learning process. Anyone who has had any experience with night schools knows that most men and women who have suddenly, or perhaps after a long period of wishful contemplation, decided to learn a foreign language will give a few evenings a week for a few months and then be bitterly disappointed if this fitful attack upon a very difficult thing like a foreign language does not yield rich results. In other words, we have generally expected more of ourselves in learning than we have expected of children, although we repeated the proverbs in self-defense when we failed.

There are serious psychological obstacles to adult study, but they cannot, since the publication of Thorndike's findings, be put down to age itself. That is, they are not to any important extent due to degenerative processes which go on in the aging mind after the attainment of physical maturity, say after the twenty-fifth year.[1] There is a decline. But it is very slight. The summation of Thorndike's work may be expressed in his own words: "We have shown that the decline from the acme of ability to learn (located probably at some point between 20 and 25) to about 42 is only about 13 to 15 per cent for a representative group of ability; and the ages 25–35 are superior to childhood, and equal or superior to early adolescence (14 to 18), in general ability to learn."

After the age of 45, according to Thorndike's results, the decline in sheer modifiability proceeds at a somewhat swifter pace, but it is Thorndike's conclusion, also, that a person should attempt to learn what he needs when he needs it, and that age should be considered an unimportant factor. This epoch-making announcement, upon which adult educators have based most of their work since, was reached after two years of careful study.

[1] The effect of decline in sensory acuity is doubtless of great importance and is now being studied.

The first thing that Thorndike and his associates wished to discover was the possible relation between the continuation of learning power and the degree of native ability. Is a long-continued power of learning associated only with high mental powers, or is the curve the same for people of all kinds? It was difficult to find existing data or to set up experiments over a sufficiently long period to determine this exactly. An ingenious study was made, however, of decline in the mental capacity with age among members of the Methodist ministry. The profession of preaching in the Methodist Church, a choice which may seem ironical to some, was selected as an unusually competitive occupation. It was found that the records of a large number of men showed that the ablest ones reached their peak of capacity at about the same age as the dullest ones. Each man passed through a curve which was of about the same shape, whether he was an eminent preacher or one of lesser brilliance.

This significant, but not conclusive study was supplemented by one of the age when various men, important enough to be recorded in a biographical dictionary, produced their greatest work. It tended to support the same conclusion, i.e., that the maximum of power comes at about the same point in a lifetime of development whether the person examined is high or low in degree of inherent ability.

The next task was consideration of the possibility of constructing a normal curve of learning capacity with relation to age. There was already available a large accumulation of data as to the power of adults to acquire certain facts, skills, and attitudes. That adults could learn was known well enough, but it was not known how well they learned at varying ages. All the available facts were studied and a number of experiments were carried out. Laboratory tests such as associations of words, calculations, and the usual tricks by which psychologists seek to unlock the mental powers of their subjects were tried out on people of all kinds and all ages.

As might have been prophesied, aging people showed noticeable decline in muscular and nervous control. In other words, there was no doubt from the beginning that if things more or less "physical" in nature were taken as the test, there was a definite degenerative decline going on with the years. Even this, however, in many types of skill was found to be not nearly so great as had been generally supposed. Throughout the long and complicated series of experiments an attempt was made to equate ability by intelligence tests and to make the data scientifically comparable. It is only with the guidance, however, of a first-rate scientific interpreter that one can get all the significance of the figures assembled.

It was discovered that "the slowness which is characteristic of old age" is not something that strikes like lightning at any particular year, but rather something which develops over a long period and very gradually. And this series of complicated experiments tended also to confirm the impression that the difficulty of adults in learning languages, even a so-called logical language like the artificial Esperanto, lies almost entirely in the loss of dexterity. Elders can, it appears, learn a language, insofar as correctness in grammar and vocabulary, instinct for idiom, and other elements are concerned, quite as well as anyone needs to, almost as well in fact as the very young. Professor Thorndike is careful to make it clear, however, that sheer "modifiability" is always greater in the first half of the third decade of life than it is at any other time.

This leads one to make a comment upon the irony of our traditional system of schooling. We put people out of school, even those who go on through college, before they have reached their full learning capacity. How often one has heard a young person say that the first few years out of college were the most interesting and, it seemed to him, the most profitable years of his life. And this is often interpreted by him and those who listen to mean that the outside world, the "great world" as it is sometimes called, is an extraordinarily interesting and real place, that school is somehow artificial, and learning an unnatural process. The findings of these scientists lead one to ask if this may not be a false interpretation of the facts.

It may be nearer truth to say that the young person between 22 and 25 would find those years the most interesting of his life no matter what he was doing at that time. If he had been working for ten years and should, by some miraculous readjustment of our school system, be allowed after a period of practical labor to devote himself and his fully grown powers entirely to the task of learning, he would find the same zest and the same astonishing adventurousness in gathering knowledge that he now finds in passing from the business of learning to the business of making a living. This is not to say, of course, that learning to make a living is an uninteresting process; on the contrary, it is very often educative in the highest sense, and the young person who goes from college into "life" is continuing to learn. But his learning in an ordinary occupation is likely to become very swiftly routinized. And it may be, as Thorndike suggests later on in his study, that the distribution of free learning time would be much more advantageous if it could be spread over a longer period.

One tends to presume that the older students who come to school because they wish to do so in order to learn things which they themselves have elected have better control over what learning powers they possess than

the young who are compelled to learn things which sometimes have no obvious meaning for them. The findings
are somewhat contrary to this supposition. It is true,
Thorndike says, that the lesser "basic modifiability" of
older people is somewhat compensated for by "better
appreciation and organization and use of what is learned,
possibly by greater interest." But there is also reason
"to believe that the older individuals are in general more
self-conscious." They do not take so readily to a novel
task. They are less hospitable to experiment. In the things
which adults really want to learn and which have a relation to the things which they have already learned in
life and are using day by day, they show much less of
this lag in learning power.

Having established that the decline in sheer learning
power from the middle twenties to the middle forties is
somewhat less than 15 per cent, a very slight loss for a
period of twenty years, the scientists under Thorndike's
leadership undertook to discover what factors actually
influence learning capacity over the span of time. These
are listed as inborn capacity, the growth of intrinsic
power which up to the time of maturity goes on independent of experience, the internal degenerative factors
which begin at the time of full maturity and are aug-
mented somewhat in the succeeding years, specific environmental factors, general environmental factors, and
the effect of the lapse of time on things already learned
but not used. This last factor is the loss of confidence
and the failure to keep active the learning already acquired.

For our purposes the most significant of all these factors
is the internal degeneration of power. It is indicated, not
definitely established, that there are no signs of rapid
degeneration with age in the learning power or inventive
capacity in other animals.

It is the opinion of Thorndike that the disuse of learning ability, that is the failure to keep on learning as a habit, is one of the things that give to every human being the impression that his mental edge dulls as he gets older. This is stated as a principle: "Adult learning is itself probably a partial method for curing adult inability to learn." Other things, then, may be more important than any physiological degenerative factors or any defects that come from age alone.

The lack of practice just mentioned is primary among the factors that affect our lives. The professional scholar, the professional practitioner of law or medicine, or of any highly learned skill who maintains his knowledge of the most recent developments in his field, and perhaps also a few other people, are the only ones who continue throughout their active careers to take learning new things, new attitudes, and new skills as normal experience. Most people who have reached the age of 30 have learned most of the things that they will ever *want* to learn. They have tried to learn other things and found either that they were not satisfied by the experience or that the game was not worth the candle. A few new gadgets may for a moment relight the flame of learning interest, but for the most part it burns low in the socket and life is a repetition of minor pleasures and minor passions which involve no great readjustments.

That this is so, and one need not be a cynic to believe it, does not in any way establish that it need be so. What is to be proved is that learning is in itself of value, and that the millions of adults who are now without that pleasure in their daily lives would enjoy it if it were added. This point, however, does not come within the statistical examination of known data nor within the range of the study of sheer learning power. It will be discussed somewhat in another place. Added to the lack of practice is the lack of time for learning. Duties of normal mature life, such as keeping house, earning a living, caring for children, and getting sufficient exercise are enough to fill most of the hours of most people.

Added to these three elements, however, lack of practice, lack of incentive, lack of time, there is another which is of a slightly different nature and which was, up to recently, left out of account. This is the absorption of energy by the necessary relearning of what we already know if we are to keep it alive. Knowledge and skill are not things that can be tied up in neat packages, labeled, and put away on shelves and then found again by some card-index system in the mind when they happen to be needed. Even people gifted with good memories find it necessary to make constant use of knowledge if it is to be kept fresh and valid.

Fortunately, most of the things which we learn are best forgotten. The miracle of forgetting is at least as marvelous as the miracle of remembering and in some ways quite as useful. A mind cluttered with exact records of all the impressions and minor experiences of every day would be a mind without organization or usefulness. The brain must constantly be sorting out, rearranging, and fortifying those things which continue to have value; this takes a certain amount of mental energy and is an obstacle to the acquisition of new things, simply because it does consume energy and time.

In one sense, then, the scientists seem to tell us, one may know and use so much that he has no time for adding to his store of knowledge. Balanced against this, there would appear to be the fact that knowledge in use is a help in the acquisition of new materials because of the systematic ways in which new things may be joined to the old and because we find significance in new ideas that come within the range of general principles already set up.

Age counts very little at least under 45, in determining whether a person will learn or fail to learn something that he sets out to get. Each human mind can acquire some things better than others, our motives differ in strength and persistence, and often in our later years we are impatient of systematic teaching and try to learn by methods of our own invention that may be inadequate for the purpose. All these things add up to much more in determining whether or not a person between 25 and 45 will learn what he wants to know than does age.

Thorndike is noncommittal as to what happens after the age of 45, but the curve of learning, as he gives it, shows that powers fail a little more rapidly after that year. He nowhere indicates that, up to the very latest years of the normal span, anyone should despair entirely of learning something that is really needed because of any fear of incapacity due to the years themselves. Since the time to learn anything is when one needs it, perhaps the answer of Cato is still the only proper one. That ancient Roman, as will be remembered, started to learn Greek when he was past eighty, and when asked why he chose to learn it at that age, he replied, "What other age have I?"

LATER INVESTIGATIONS

The publication of *Adult Learning* was a heartening confirmation of the working faith of pioneers. Later researches have tempered enthusiasm somewhat but have not changed the basic principle, that age is not a bar to further learning. Thorndike's own more recent books have indicated two fundamental elements in method by showing that learning by adults is slower than learning by the young, and that mature persons are more easily discouraged.

Weisenburg, Roe, and McBride have summarized compactly the whole range of studies by numerous investigators in adult intelligence, including learning power specifically. Their conclusion is "that by far the greatest extent of mental development as indicated by these test performances has occurred before the twenties, and that from this decade through the fifties there is little further gain and comparatively little decline."[1] More important as a contribution is their finding that "the peak of development and the course with age are different for different performances." This "course with age" means change in abilities of different sorts at succeeding age levels. It is indicated again that the pace of learning is slower as the student grows older. Abilities involving the use of words appear to decline less than others.

The important methodological conclusion that the adult needs more time for learning is further confirmed by Irving Lorge who has been associated with Thorndike in much of his investigation. In various papers, several of which are not yet published, Lorge has shown that mental tests are more significant with regard to age if those which involve speed are distinguished from those which do not. By making such a distinction one can conclude that reported "curves" of mental decline are often more accurately described as curves measuring the slowing up of reaction time, co-ordination, speed, and sensory acuity.

The psychologists, in other words, are offering no evidence that men and women do not grow old and, in aging, lose some of their powers. What they do offer, with increasing completeness, is a guide to the powers which can be maintained. The mature person has ambitions that are different from those that stirred him in

[1] *Adult Intelligence*, The Commonwealth Fund, 1936, p. 125.

youth. If one of these ambitions is to learn more of the world in which he lives and better answers to the problems of his time, his years will be less important than other qualities of mind and character in determining his success.

Questions for Discussion

1. Give a brief account of your own habits of study at the age of 15. At 20. At present. If they have changed, can you tell why?

2. Give a sketch of the daily program, outside of time spent in earning a living, of two of your friends who have continued to seek learning after the age of 25. Contrast this with the customary activities of some of your friends who seem to you to have ceased learning.

3. Can you find any flaws in the case made out for the "learning curve" given in Thorndike's *Adult Learning?*

4. Can you distinguish between "intellectual" and "psychological" elements in learning?

5. If you had the scientific skill and equipment necessary for further investigation of the powers of the adult mind, what would you seek to find out?

Reading References

Lorge, Irving, "The Influence of Tests upon the Nature of Mental Decline as a Function of Age," *Journal of Educational Psychology*, Vol. XXVII, pp. 100-110, February, 1936.

SORENSON, HERBERT, *Adult Abilities in Extension Classes*, The University of Minnesota Press, 1933.

STRONG, E. K., *Change of Interest with Age*, Stanford University Press, 1931.

THORNDIKE, E. L., and others, *Adult Learning*, The Macmillan Company, 1928.

THORNDIKE, E. L., *Adult Interests*, The Macmillan Company, 1935.

THORNDIKE, E. L., *The Psychology of Wants, Interests and Attitudes*, D. Appleton-Century Co., 1935.

WEISENBURG, ROE, and MCBRIDE, *Adult Intelligence*, The Commonwealth Fund, 1936.

Chapter Five

THE ROLE OF THE TEACHER IN ADULT EDUCATION

THE RESPONSIBILITIES of a teacher of adults are much the same as those of any other teacher. He can often make the rough places plain, and he can sometimes sharpen difficulties when he considers that a student needs the shock of perplexity to awaken him. He can supplement the dry bones of a text with the flesh of concrete instances taken from the immediate experience of those with whom he is studying. And he can, of course, be the regulator who maintains the intellectual framework of the subject by which the students make their efforts systematic. He has other responsibilities, however, which although not different from those of the teacher of the young are perhaps more important in his position. He will make any study in any subject, no matter what may be the student's interest in self-education, an enticement to further learning. Second, he will inculcate by example and by constant alert guidance, the principles of a rational skepticism. Third, he may sometimes, at his peril, take on the role of leader.

The first duty is limited only by the breadth of his own interests and the vitality of his own intellectual life. It is not limited by the subject which he is asked to teach. As has been said, the motives of those who come to formal or informal adult-learning opportunities may be mixed in emphasis, but they are always single in fundamentals. No matter what one comes to study or practice, what he really desires is the enlargement of himself. A machinist who studies blue-print reading, a typist who asks that she be taught greater speed or skill with the typewriter, a woman who wants to know how to make her own hats or dresses, all these are seeking fundamentally a better means of self-expression, even though they may translate that directly into a higher wage or an economic advantage. We have already said that the sharp division between occupational and liberal studies is falsely drawn. Learning to speak English when one is of foreign birth, or acquiring the elements of knowledge of American institutions which will enable a man to become a naturalized citizen, these also are of the same nature. They are for self-improvement.

When one begins with the principle that adult education is self-education, that it starts with the student where he is and takes him in the direction in which he wishes to go, any beginning is as good as any other, provided the teacher is good enough. If the teacher centers his own interest and concern upon the student rather than upon the thing studied, it matters very little what the student begins with. The result should always be the same, namely, a desire for further learning and further self-development. The unrevealed powers and undeveloped potentialities of people may be unlocked by many different keys. As long as adult education is kept free of such measures of success as are outside the student's own self, and is true to its ideal purpose of being worth while for its own sake, any teacher of any subject can very well carry on his exploration of that subject and his association with the student who has chosen it in such a way as to lead into wider and wider interests.

To defend the statement that it is also one of the chief

responsibilities of a teacher of adults to exemplify and teach a rational skepticism requires, perhaps, more argument. It brings us dangerously close to that most confused of all educational questions, shall we indoctrinate? Here one may draw a proper distinction between adult education and all other forms of the educational process. To recall what was said in an earlier chapter, the chief business of elementary education and, in these modern times, part of the business of secondary schooling, is the necessary one of transferring to each member of the new generation the cultural accumulation which he must master if he is to live as a member of a normal society. This is a part of, indeed one of the chief elements in the experience by which he can develop his own personality. The school is the social device by which a very necessary task is performed. If it is unsuccessfully done, the students are homeless in a strange world, and society lacks the units of support which make up its structure.

There is still room, of course, for criticism and reconstruction in the schooling process of the young, but these are not primary for them. They can scarcely criticize or reconstruct a society which they have not first come to understand. It is not only possible but necessary for the superintendent of the schools of any city to say in effect to all of the children of that city: "Here are certain things which you must learn if you are to be members of this social group. You may not now see the necessity for them, but you must, until you are mature, trust our experience and wisdom to define some of these things for you. Otherwise, when you are old enough to meet social problems, you will not be prepared for your own part in the world's work." The wise teacher will struggle to confine this compulsion to those "tool" subjects where it is justified.

The adult student comes with quite a different attitude and for quite a different purpose. He has already adapted his personality, more or less successfully, to the interplay between himself and his environment. He knows the patterns of his culture. In fact, he comes to school either because he cannot adjust himself to those patterns satisfactorily, or because he wishes to acquire some power with which to change them. No one can say to him, "Here are things that you must learn." Even the wisest can only advise him. And his educational needs include more than the acquiring of greater economic skill and the special knowledge that appeals to him. He needs also to find guidance in the whirl of opinions and ideas and pressures which bear down upon him. In fact, his greatest social need is to learn not how to acquire but to resist, to stand firmly against the winds of doctrine, to choose in a bewildering plenty of suggestions and advice and propaganda those things which will best serve his own purposes and advance him in his own development.

In a civilization like ours, the arts of the merchant are much more refined and skillful than those of any other common practitioner, and they are generally practiced in the realm of ideas and politics as well as in the selling of mere things. Consequently, the negative logic of skepticism is a very necessary part of a healthy personality. The educator of adults serves this purpose, first, by giving a steady example of thinking which is not only careful and related to ascertainable facts, but also critical in nature. That is, thinking which examines all the stuff in any argument without regard for prejudice or faith and with the least possible emotional inclination.

If the teacher is himself careful in arriving at conclusions, respectful of facts when they can be had, and tolerant of all points of view contrary to his own, he is not only fulfilling the first phase of this task, he is also laying the foundation for further steps. If he can demonstrate the freedom and reasonableness of his own thinking, he can more safely undertake to point out mistakes in the thinking of his students. He will be trusted and to some extent tolerated when he undertakes to show that prejudice is prejudice and nothing more, or refuses to accept popular ideas merely because they are popular; when he insists in cool good humor upon digging underneath all conclusions, particularly when they are made with the heat that betrays their shaky foundations. He can even dare to question absolutes and insist upon the relativity of truth, which is the mark of the scientific method. It would be too sanguine to suppose that this task is ever easy for the teacher in his own thinking. It is even more difficult when he attempts to spread his own scientific skepticism to his associates in the adult classroom or the public forum. It is obviously easier in some areas than in others, and the wise teacher will know when to press the painful scalpel of doubt and when to agree in form if not in substance. But a constant and stubborn effort to help those students who work with him to acquire a more alert attitude toward their already accepted and verbalized beliefs, and toward all new things offered them, is the hallmark of a fit teacher for grown men and women.

This assertion that the cultivation of a rational skepticism in himself and in his students is a primary obligation of the educator of adults leads necessarily to some consideration of another question. In what degree and in what way is the teacher of adults a leader? A dominating personality moves naturally and with most ease in rather crude simplifications of questions which by their nature are complex. As the politician is gifted in making slogans that express nearly all the truth about a great issue, so the lecturer, the forum leader, the teacher must be able to simplify.

In all social processes, leaders are necessary. And a

leader who cannot produce action is no leader at all. Just what role a man or woman will play in the complicated social affairs of his time and place is a matter for each person to decide for himself, and the teacher of adults has the same opportunity and freedom in this regard as any other person. But he cannot successfully discharge his teaching function if he does not define for himself very clearly in the beginning, and in regard to each phase of his work, just what his attitude toward action is going to be. The word "education" is used so loosely, one might almost say so shamelessly, to apply to all kinds of social coercion and appeal, that every teacher, whether of adults or youth, must necessarily have a clear picture of what he is trying to do.

Adult education is part of a social movement which needs two kinds of people. Argument as to which is more useful would be a waste of time, since both are necessary. It is a social movement and has social ends. We hope that action will eventually come from clear thinking and mutual enlightenment. There must be some leaders who will crystallize thought into those cruder and more simple forms by which men can move steadily toward overt results. As has been pointed out (by Bertrand Russell, for example), we never can act or hope to act from complete knowledge. When the time for action comes, we must necessarily work with what we have. And one might add that it is not only necessary to act before complete understanding has been attained, it is also necessary to act upon some statement of the issues involved which we know does violence to part of the truth. Action is not a matter of more or less, it is always a matter of yes or no. Logic necessarily leads us to the more or less position. Those who are natural leaders in society deal comfortably with the simplicities and the slogans. They dominate because of their faith in these

ways of thinking and because of their skill in inventing
the verbal symbols which move men's minds and hearts.

Those who have the temperament and intellectual
qualities which make this kind of leadership natural and
possible to them have a place in the social movement for
progress of which adult education is a part. They are
not the best teachers. Teaching is not their native function. But they are needed and they are not likely to be
lacking.

Men are prone to action. It is a philosopher's fallacy
produced in the ivory tower of his remote acquaintance
with the practical world to suppose that men need to be
urged to act. What they need is wisdom before they act.
Almost from the beginning of rational thought, at least
so far as it is recorded, philosophers have been endeavor-
ing to get men to act upon the basis of reason rather
than to move first and use their reasoning powers for
justification afterward. It would be folly to pretend
that any large number of men in any civilization have
attained to this deliberate method. It is implicit in all
scientific work, but even scientists display no great desire to use it outside the laboratory, and in the social
sciences it is noticeably lacking even in what passes for
strict methodological operation. In adult education,
there is surely a place for a further struggle to slow down
man's precipitate and thoughtless speed in action to the
end that he may, in the calm interval, attain a clearer
definition of his purposes and a clearer vision of the consequences. The fundamental questioning of all things,
which began far back in the history of Western thought
and reached its greatest expression in the Socratic dia-
logues of Plato, is as necessary and as rare in modern
times as it ever was.

The one to whom we can give the name of teacher is
he who will maintain in his own thinking, and against

the hurried simplifications of more dominant and less intellectual leaders, the skepticism that serves as a social corrective. One who undertakes to play this role, however, must accept without complaint the fact that he does by his very temperament and procedure put himself in direct contravention, not only to others in the educational world but to all the natural leaders of the social process, who will dislike him because he is skeptical, who will accuse him of cowardice because he urges deliberation, who will ridicule his science and his wisdom because they produce no easy answers. Those who have this philosophic desire are used to that difficulty and can abide in it.

Even though we can establish this distinction between teaching and leading, we must allow that many workers in the field play both roles, *not at once*, but in relation to different students, or at different times, or in different activities. Even what we have here called "teaching" earns a moral authority for leadership which cannot be disclaimed. The good teacher keeps his responsibility clear in his own mind. He endeavors to see that every seeker after knowledge finds somehow and somewhere both the dispassionate guidance that makes his purposes clear and the leader who will inspire him to free action.

QUESTIONS FOR DISCUSSION

1. At what stage in the school experience of a child would you begin to encourage him to question existing social, political, and economic ideas?

2. Does criticism without shared responsibility have educational value?

3. What effect do you think running for political office would have on the professional qualities of a teacher?

Do you think this experience would be of the same significance for a teacher in the secondary schools as for a forum leader?

4. What are the chief intellectual qualities of political leaders whom you have known or whose lives you have studied?

5. Do you have access to unbiased information on any important political, economic, or social question? How do you arrive at your own opinions in such matters? Describe what you believe to be the habits of your friends and acquaintances in reaching decisions for action on public questions.

READING REFERENCES

CARTWRIGHT, MORSE A., *Ten Years of Adult Education*, The Macmillan Company, Chaps. V, VI, VII, and XI.

JOHNSON, ALVIN S., *Deliver Us from Dogma*, American Association for Adult Education, 1934.

KILPATRICK, W. H., "The Task Confronting Adult Education," *Journal of Adult Education*, Vol. I, No. 4, October, 1929.

KOTINSKY, RUTH, *Adult Education and the Social Scene*, D. Appleton-Century Co. Part III, Chap. VII.

MARTIN, EVERETT DEAN, *The Meaning of a Liberal Education*, W. W. Norton and Company, 1926.

RUSSELL, BERTRAND, *Education and the Modern World*, W. W. Norton and Company, 1932.

Chapter Six

HOW ADULTS CAN BE TAUGHT

ANY SITUATION which puts one adult mind into fruitful co-operation with another is, in one sense, adult education. We are concerned here, however, with the more or less formal arrangements by which a teacher is confronted with students, whether the teacher-pupil relation is accepted or reduced in a spirit of equality to its least possible significance. We can all learn from one another, but whenever one accepts responsibility for teaching he has need of method. If all those who know what others would like to know were geniuses in communicating thought, there would be no need for system or for pedagogy. Method is the only substitute for divine inspiration. Knowledge of method distinguishes the professional from the amateur.

One who undertakes to teach adults should know the psychology of the learning process and the principles of some accepted system of pedagogy. These he should keep loosely in hand so that he may readily adapt them to what he learns from his own experience. It is far too soon to dogmatize on the best ways of stimulating the mature mind to new ideas or of adding new skills to the mature personality. Whatever is said must be tentative. We shall try only to state what appears now to be the best practice, first in classwork, then in various types of adult learning groups.

In every form of adult study and adult self-education, there are special advantages and disadvantages. In elementary work, in which the aim is remedial, the greatest advantage and some danger are in the fact that the learner is seldom inclined to dispute the authority of text or teacher. The rules of English grammar, or the meaning of the Constitution as it must be accepted for citizenship, and even simple skills in homemaking are likely to be accepted without question. The characteristic freedom of adult study is here at a minimum. This is not to say that things will be easily learned, but only that the learner's own opinions are not among the obstacles which learning has to overcome. These obstacles lie rather in habit, inhibitions, and the sheer difficulty of new intellectual experience. If the essence of method is an understanding of the student's difficulties and a respect for his powers, we may start with what we know of the handicaps and capacities of the average mature mind.

An understanding of the student's difficulties is not all that is required. There must also be sufficient respect for his powers and sufficient sympathy with his purposes to make the teacher's knowledge of these difficulties a means of helping him to overcome them.

The first necessity, then, in dealing with adult students on the elementary level, is to understand their difficulties so well that they may make the greatest possible progress and avoid unnecessary defeat or discouragement.

This will necessitate two restrictions upon the teacher: one, as to speed; the other, as to units or divisions of subject matter. If adults can learn approximately as well but never as rapidly as they could when they were children, teaching must be adjusted to their optimum speed. The teacher who has had classroom experience with children is especially likely to go wrong in this regard. She has discovered that a certain amount of psychological pressure will make children work harder and bring results. The circumstances of the child's classroom are such that learning can be made a task. It is not best done in this way, but it can be compelled by pressure. The goals of learning may be set up and the child pushed toward them. Pressure from the teacher is exerted in such a way as to make the child afraid of failure rather than hopeful of success. It would be impossible, of course, to estimate how much teaching of this sort now exists in American schoolrooms, but that it is traditional cannot be doubted, and that it is general seems very likely. When the pupil is an adult, it is disastrous. A mature man or woman who has publicly admitted that he cannot read and write, and has offered his effort and his free time in the hope of curing that deficiency, needs no compulsion. Many teachers of adults err in their enforcement of childish discipline, in their impatience, and in their condescension, but even these are less serious than hurrying pressure.

Instead of standing behind people and pushing them toward predetermined goals, the successful teacher of adults, especially on the adult elementary level, is a leader along a journey which has well-defined and frequent landmarks. This is the second restriction on the teacher: that he must work in short units. The teacher leads along this graded series with a constant mindfulness of the speed possible to his sensitive and easily discouraged student. And he takes every opportunity of pointing out that another milestone has been passed. This gives to the adult student a frequently recurring sense of achievement. Nothing else will sustain him.

The teacher of adults on the elementary level is mindful also of the fact that study is a habit which for most of us is learned in childhood. After being learned, as is unhappily too evident, it can quickly be forgotten and even those who once possessed it find some barriers to getting it back. Many of the adult students on the elementary level have never acquired such a habit. Their school experience was too short for them to learn the close concentration on academic problems which makes for scholastic accomplishment. For this reason, what has just been said of the necessity for a frequently recurring sense of achievement, that is, such a method of instruction as will give them in generous plenty the feeling that they are making progress, is seen to be of paramount importance. And because concentration is genuinely difficult, there should be frequent changes of activity in order to avoid weariness and boredom.

The teacher of adults will be wise to remember that stamina is of various kinds and that the special kind of stamina which shows in the capacity for sustained mental effort is one that has not often been acquired by people whose educational experience is deficient. They must have in its place a kind of courage which is a moral quality rather than an intellectual one. If these students are deficient not because of some failure in the social system to give them in their youth the opportunity for a minimum education, but rather because of some intellectual defect, then what has here been said becomes even more emphatic. The mistake of the inexperienced teacher in dealing with adults, however, is rather to suppose that slowness in comprehension is stupidity, when as a matter of fact it may be educational inexperience.

Aside from these general attitudes the teacher of adults on the elementary level must be possessed of endless devices for classroom use. Many of these are set forth in available manuals. A teacher with imagination can indefinitely extend experiments in finding new approaches to old problems. In doing so, he will naturally learn as much as he can about the daily life and experiences of the people whom he is trying to teach in order that materials offered them may have concrete reality.

These considerations of method do not contradict in any way what was said earlier about the main consideration in the teaching of adults on this level, which is to make all newly acquired knowledge an open door to expanding intellectual experience. If they are learning successfully, that is to say happily, they are acquiring the most valuable of all knowledge, which is that learning itself is a pleasure. They are acquiring at the same time both a tool and a desire to use it.

CLASSWORK ON THE HIGHER LEVELS

When all the facts concerning the psychology of adult learning and the motives which lead men and women to pursue intellectual activities are taken into account, there is very little more to be said about methods of teaching the ordinary subjects in formal classwork. How much the future development of the movement will involve the expansion of classwork on the higher levels cannot now be predicted. University extension has been almost entirely of this sort, and it has to a very large extent done no more and no less than to move the college-class technique into a new place or to move a new kind of class into the college hall.

Flexibility of method on the higher levels becomes more and more a matter of necessity if one is to be successful and if the studies taken up are subjective in their content and normative in their principles. Many subjects even on the highest levels may be taught very much as are common branches on the elementary level. If the subjects are such as must be accepted on the authority of the teacher or the textbook, a professor of one of the exact sciences who is fortunate enough to have a class of adults will be governed largely by the same considerations as govern the methods of the teacher of elementary subjects. He will be constrained to remember that the people with whom he is dealing, however intelligent and however interested, are not as well accustomed to concentrated study as are his college undergraduates. But he will not need to take into account their opinions.

In the field of the social sciences, however, the student's opinion becomes more and more an important element in the learning process. It may be said that even the social sciences, insofar as they are scientifically perfected, are matters of exact knowledge; but in these sciences, and even more in philosophy and in the arts, the interpretation of facts is a major element in learning, and adult students do not take kindly to authoritarian teaching. Perhaps it would be better to say that the more intelligent and worth-while adult students do not ever take kindly to authoritarian teaching. A certain docility under instruction is characteristic of many mature men and women; in fact, it has been said that the more education they have had the more docile they are. Whether this willingness to accept as gospel what any teacher or any book may say is due to faulty schooling or to intrinsic human tendencies is a matter not to be decided here. It need only be said that the more able and independent the students happen to be, the more they will be inclined to pitch their own experience and knowledge against that of the teacher. The good teacher welcomes this independence.

There is reason to believe that the most important

phases of adult education are those in which the opinions
of the students have the same right to expression as have
the opinions of the teacher, provided that they are cheerfully offered for the logical examination and the factual
test of classroom discussion. It can doubtless be said that
these considerations apply to all kinds of teaching. To
state them here is an acknowledgment of the fact that,
although useful in all kinds of teaching, they are frequently absent. In adult education they are more than
ever necessary.

QUESTIONS FOR DISCUSSION

1. What would you logically expect to be the chief differences between methods satisfactory in dealing with
   children and those that work well with adults?

2. Take a chapter of a high-school text in history and
   plan a series of assignments for adults of average
   school experience.

3. It is often said that the average school experience of
   the American adult population is not more than the
   eighth grade. Discuss this in the light of your own
   impressions of the general public. What "out-of-
   school" experiences would have contributed most to
   the attitudes, skills, and ideas of these mature people?

4. What can a teacher do for the adult student who has
   access to books on the subjects he wishes to study?

5. Analyze the qualities of the teacher who has done
   most for you in college. Would his methods have
   brought the same response if you had been under his
   guidance in a group outside the college system, not
   working for credit?

Reading References

Mackaye, David L., "Tactical Training for Teaching Adults," *Journal of Adult Education*, Vol. III, No. 3, June, 1931.

Payson and Haley, *Adult Education in Homemaking*, D. Appleton-Century Co., 1929.

Thorndike, E. L., *Adult Interests*, The Macmillan Company, 1935.

Whipple, Guyton, and Morriss, *Manual for Teachers of Adult Elementary Students*, American Association for Adult Education, 1935.

Chapter Seven

SPECIAL METHODS

ALL METHODS in adult education are more or less informal. Every group is made up of people differing in
experience and in preparation. The average mature person will dislike the regimentation of the old-fashioned
class, even though he may be docile to authoritarian
teaching. Informality is necessary. Some of the less formal ways of reaching the learner's response are worthy
of extended examination.

It is not possible, however, to relate classwork or the
informal methods exactly to the functional types of adult
education. In general, we may say that regular classes
will be used for the most part in remedial work. Classes
with the shop as a laboratory will be the basic method in
occupational training. The discussion group is perhaps
the most useful form for organizing relational work. In
liberal studies all methods are useful. In political education the lecture, the discussion group, and the forum,
which is a combination of the two, are generally relied
on. In all work with and for adults, all methods should
be put into practice if they offer any advantage for a
special phase of the student's experience.

Lectures, discussion groups, forums, and radio broadcasting are adaptations of the teacher's verbal appeal to
the student's mind. Laboratory and studio put the learner
in direct contact with tangible materials. Correspondence

gives to the teacher a ghostly but effective reality in the student's thinking. His own reading supplements all the other stimuli to which he may be subjected.

THE LECTURE

The "lecture" has been under fire. Doubt as to the effectiveness of this method of imparting information and inducing learning has been current among educational theorists for a decade or more. In spite of the fact that the lecture is still the favorite method in scholastic halls and, further, that it is still a favorite intellectual recreation for vast numbers of American people, particularly clubwomen, it has been called a good many harsh names.

As a form of teaching in the classroom, the lecture has no doubt been misused. It is a practical device for getting large numbers of undergraduates into slight contact with a distinguished teacher, when common sense would indicate that closer contact with some less famous tutor would probably arouse more genuine activity. If it were not for obvious economic difficulties, one might say that beginning classes should always be organized in small groups under careful supervision, and that classes should grow larger, and be subjected more and more to lectures, as the students go further in their knowledge of the subject.

The use of the lecture in adult classes, however, differs in important ways from its use in the classroom. Whatever may be said for and against the method when dealing with college or high-school students is true when it is used with adults. In non-scholastic programs, the lecture is and probably always will be of primary importance. In the first place, the lecturer is useful because he can arouse interest in a subject and in adult education in general. As long as people are busy with the cares of daily life, as long as many of them are shy of arduous mental labor pursued on their own time, and particularly as long as many of them have a strong curiosity about the appearance and personality of famous or distinguished people, the lecturer has drawing power. One may be tolerant or contemptuous of the amount of genuine thinking which mere attendance at a lecture by a famous person may produce, but he cannot, if he is practical, overlook the fact that many people who begin by going to more or less superficial lectures remain to study or go elsewhere to read. As a method of arousing interest in continuing learning, then, the lecturer has a definite function and uses a method which nothing else can quite replace.

Even people who are far removed from mere curiosity-seeking, indeed many of those who have studied faithfully along some lines of interest, can find in lectures on new subjects an exploratory experience. They can, through attendance at lectures, expose themselves to new kinds of knowledge. The lecturer, if he is passably good, can give a warmth and variety to the treatment of a new subject which few books supply, and above all he can give a conspectus of the important elements of a subject in briefer and more appealing form than can, except in rare instances, be got from books. Thus even the more serious students will sometimes find an entirely new line of inquiry opened up by a talk.

Some defense can also be made for the lecture method as a saving of time. It may be that those who go to lectures rather than to books and periodicals for information and illuminating comment are most anxious to save themselves effort. This does not change the fact, however, that busy people often get from a lecture a quick summary of what might otherwise be inaccessible.

Even if it be true that many people go to lectures without listening alertly and without taking much away, some consideration must be given to the art of lecturing itself, since it ought fairly to be said that if talks are a waste of time it is almost always because they are given without skill.

To be educationally effective in the occasional talk is difficult. The academic authority, whose attitude is far too often tainted with the notion that he is going on a slumming party, is not enough interested in being understood. He has no time and energy for studying the viewpoint of the people to whom he is talking and for adapting his more or less erudite material to their immediate need. He may even choose to be obscure in the hope that that will make him seem more learned. These strictures may seem ungrateful to many of the college teachers who have for years worked valiantly for the cause of popular education and have made sacrifices to bring the fruits of their learning to the service of the public at large. But if lecturing is considered an incidental addition to a faculty income rather than one of the most difficult forms of teaching, a good deal of it must be without educational value.

Praise is gladly given to those statesmen who use the lecture platform as a place for explaining their policies to the people, to those authors who open new worlds to the imagination of auditors, to those explorers and scientists who open wider worlds to the experience of the general public, and to those competent journalists who prefer an oral medium to the printed word for the discussion of current affairs. These people cannot, of course, hope to achieve in casual and infrequent contact with audiences anything like the cumulative effect of teaching or orderly reading. Many of them, however, do bring memorable experiences to vast numbers of people. To say that they do not stimulate and instruct, that they are not contributing to adult education, would be unreasonable and untrue.

The current questioning of lecturing as a method comes not from lack of appreciation for the work done by the better people of both these groups, the academic and the popular. It is caused, first, by the extent to which lecturing has been degraded from its intellectual dignity by charlatans and camp followers of the great; second, by a realization that, no matter how spirited a stimulus may be given by a lecture, unless something further is done by the recipients of that stimulus, its effect wears quickly away and leaves no trace.

If lecturing is bad, nothing can be said for it. If it is good, it is mostly a stimulus. The great need is to build upon this impulse such devices as will make good use of it and lead to lasting effect. When lectures are followed by the use of reading lists, when subjects begun in lectures are carried on in small study groups, when discussion, as in the better types of forums, can explicate and expand the lecturer's thought and make it more personal to at least some of the hearers, that is to say, when the stimulus leads to further intellectual effort, the effect is something worth having. The wise educator of adults does not disregard the use of lectures for their stimulating and exploratory value. He sees to it that vivid and colorful exponents of great ideas have a chance to get a hearing. But he tries to build from these things the after-efforts which make them genuinely educational.

DISCUSSION

The general informality of adult learning has led to a considerable use of what is called the "discussion method."

Discussion can be developed into a fine art if its techniques are taken seriously enough and practiced carefully enough by those who would master them. A knowledge of what makes a discussion satisfactory is useful to any teacher of adults who often finds himself in informal situations. Some literature has been produced that undertakes to instruct inexperienced people in leading discussions. A part of this literature is helpful, but much is too highly formalized to be of value. And much of it sets up highly artificial requirements for success. There are "rules," such as that people cannot "discuss" unless the group is very small and every member takes an active part in the talk. Persons brought together with a self-conscious purpose may subject themselves to such limitations, but for the practical worker in adult education a much more flexible conception of discussion is necessary.

It is useful for the leader or teacher to know what subjects can be fruitfully "discussed" and which are best attacked in other ways. He should know some of the qualities by which discussion can be judged. It is useful for him to realize that discussion is often illuminating to all the members of a group even though they do not all take an active part in it; in other words, that one may participate intellectually without expressing any opinions aloud. It is equally important for him to realize that, if discussion is to be a method in education, many people will have to become gradually acquainted with it. They will have to occupy positions on the edge of the talk for a considerable period before they are equipped to enter into it. It is quite unnecessary to exclude people from a group because they are not already experts in the fine art of dialectic.

Much abuse has been piled on the discussion method in the last few years since it has become popular. It has been called "pooled ignorance." The question is sometimes asked, Why should anyone discuss a problem when all he needs to do is to find someone who knows the answer and ask for it? Some of this criticism has been deserved, because the method has often been used for purposes to which it is very ill adapted. It is not a sensible use of the discussion method to apply it to questions which can be better answered by ascertainable facts. Nor is pooled opinion, even if it be not entirely pooled ignorance, a substitute for authoritative opinion.

The mistake has been in using discussion when questions that can be decided by either fact or authority have been at issue. The most important decisions which human beings have to make, however, and the most important problems which they wish to consider in any adult-learning process cannot be settled by either fact or authority. Serious arguments as to questions of ethics, politics, economics, and social affairs begin after all the available facts are in hand. And it is to these questions which involve every man's judgment, and about which every man has a right to his own reasonable opinion, that the discussion method is properly applied.

This means that discussion, when it is a useful learning process, or a useful method of adult education, is essentially an argument about individual judgments. It is the exchange of opinion about propositions which are seldom if ever to be answered by yes or no but rather to be balanced by more or less. The discussion method is of little use in studying physics or astronomy. It cannot do much with the mere facts even of the social sciences, such as history or economics. But the use of the facts in subjects such as history or economics in adult education is only to form the springboard for individual thinking, that is, for judgments upon the facts.

In political education the discussion method is of primary importance. It is not education for a mature man to accept from the lips of any authority, or from any uninterpreted tabulation of facts, his final political opinion. With all decent respect for the truth which will lead him to base his own thinking upon all facts available, and with all due responsiveness to the wisdom of those he considers his betters, he will still have to make up his mind for himself. One seldom knows the strength or weakness of his own opinion until he has attempted to express it in friendly and tolerant talk, has discovered what others think on the same subject, and has pursued the conversation until some kind of adjustment is made between what he thinks and what his fellows appear to think. Discussion, then, if it can be free and tolerant but at the same time keen and to the point, is the only method for accomplishing these educational ends.

Since discussion as a learning or a teaching method is useful because it stimulates the expression and clarification of individual opinion, group sessions need not necessarily end in agreement. There are groups, of course, such as committees and other "action" organizations, which use discussion as a means of arriving at decisions. If a decision or some sort of action must necessarily eventuate, agreement becomes in that same degree necessary. Individual stimulation and learning can be achieved without agreement and without action.

This again brings us to a moot point in modern education. Is it of any value to any man to learn something upon which he does not act? The problem has evoked a good deal of shallow thinking and loud speech from people who seem to believe that action is the chief end of man even if it be unintelligent and disastrous in practical result. Pertinent questions are, Action when? What kind of action? A discussion group should be judged like any other human activity, not as if it were a single

and entirely closed experience but as a part of the lives of
those who participate in it. They are not born on the
doorstep of the discussion group, nor do they die on the
way out. Something learned in friendly converse with
other students may find its final justification in action
which takes place years afterward. A changed point of
view on a controversial question is as important as a
rush to do something before a question is really understood. Pericles boasted that his Athenians were no less
valiant in battle because they deliberated on their com-
paigns.

And what kind of action? Men are not loath to act.
In politics, in social affairs, in practical economics,
they move, and for the most part they have always
moved, with very little acquaintance with available facts,
and with almost no rational thought concerning their
import. The chief business of adult education is to per-
suade men to use intelligence in all their serious affairs.
Then the necessary effect of more and better adult education will be to slow up action, not to hasten it, in the
hope that when it comes, as it inevitably must, it will
be more nearly a fair reflection of the judgment of the
people.

Discussion is a solvent of prejudice and of hasty response to propaganda. As one of the methodological instruments of adult education it cannot be judged by its
immediate results in either agreement or practical application. It has been successful for each person who has
taken part insofar as it has roused his mind, broadened
his powers, and clarified his opinions.

If it is to accomplish these results, discussion cannot be
merely *about* a subject. It must be on an issue. In other
words, it is essentially controversy. Discussion arises actually out of differences of opinion in regard to things
about which men have the right to hold opinions. It may

degenerate on the one side into mere aimless talk from which no issue emerges, or on the other into debate in which participants are trying to score off one another rather than to discover the truth. The middle ground is sometimes hard to find.

A skilled leader is needed, something more and something less than a teacher. The leader is less than a teacher in that he need not necessarily know more about the subject under consideration than other members of his group. He is more than a teacher in the fact that by the use of a very difficult art he is creating something new out of the thought and speech of those whom he is guiding in talk.

Primary principles of method for the leader of discussion may be summarized:

1. The leader must know the purpose of his group. If the members meet together only to explore a subject and their various opinions, his duties are very different from what they are for a group who have a definite mandate to arrive at a decision and to do something about it. The leader of a learning group has a very different task from the chairman of a committee. He will see that the group accomplishes its purpose and will not force it into something which is not necessary to that purpose.

2. He will have clearly in mind, and will keep clearly in the minds of the members of his group, the issue that is being discussed. Without being a disciplinarian, he must see that the speakers stick to the subject unless by common agreement an original subject is abandoned and a new proposition taken up.

3. He will respond hospitably to the contributions of all the persons in the group. He will make sure that every contribution is heard and understood and that it is woven into the common thought.

4. He will remember what is said, not only to save

time but also to make the cumulative pattern of thought which is the real purpose of the meeting.

5. Because he can remember and think clearly and express himself well, he will frequently summarize and point out the direction which the talk is taking.

Even the best of leaders will not be able usually to content those critics who object to every discussion because they are not genuinely interested in the opinions of others. Nor will he be able to content those who think that all important questions have easy answers which can be simply stated and immediately put into effect. But he can help honest people to express honest opinions and help them get a hearing. He can help the inarticulate and encourage the thoughtful but timid ones. He can give pleasure to those of keen mind who find pleasure in dialectic or the clash of ideas. He can help in the formation of that public opinion which is at bottom the controlling influence in a free government.

Because the method has such great possibilities and is at the same time so difficult, careful study of the techniques is essential to the well-rounded equipment of any educator of adults. For the most part, the best practitioners of this method have been, like the best practitioners of all other adult-education methods, entirely self-taught. They have learned tact and have discarded devices that blocked free talk or led to triviality and tedium. And in a very real sense discussion leading can only be learned from experience. It is essentially an art and not a science, to be acquired by watching the performance of the adept and by studying one's own mistakes rather than by learning rules. All art can be learned in some degree, however, and the study of techniques will improve the methods of any leader in adult education or any teacher in a classroom where he faces mature men and women. As must be pointed out over and over again, because it is fundamental to every methodological consideration in this field, the students here considered not only have opinions but have a right to express them. A knowledge of how to sharpen and point up the conversation of an informal classroom to lead it to the available and pertinent facts, to imbue it at the same time with the spirit of friendliness and tolerance, to show by example how to talk straight and think hard—these are all fundamental elements in the making of a good teacher of mature minds.

The perfect discussion leader, if one could ever exist, would deserve the description which Bishop Westcott once wrote of Henry Sidgwick: "Great in range and exactness of knowledge, great in subtlety of analysis, great in power of criticism, he offered the highest type of a seeker of the truth, more anxious to understand an opponent's argument than to refute him; watchful lest any element in a discussion should be unnoticed, patient, reverent, ready to the last to welcome light from any quarter." [1]

And a sense of humor.

THE FORUM

The forum method is in substance a lecture followed by a question-and-discussion period. It is one of the best methods for dealing with controversial questions in politics, economics, or public affairs. In all the various ways of organizing forum programs the purpose remains the same, to subject listeners to differing points of view, from which they may choose for themselves.

Should a forum "leader" be a frank advocate of what he thinks is the best solution of a question? Should he be

[1] John Morley, *Recollections*, Macmillan, 1917, Vol. I, p. 123.

"non-partisan"? Should he state all sides of a question as well as he can and then state his own preferences?

The "non-partisan" attitude is often urged upon the leader as a scholarly duty. Is it possible? We have already said that the teacher of adults has the duty of critical—even skeptical—thinking. He must be watchful for flaws in his own logic and ready to change his own ideas when he finds something better. But a genuine non-partisan attitude would be a genuine indifference. A pretended non-partisan attitude would be a deception, certainly deceiving to his hearers, possibly to himself.

Should the forum speaker then be always an advocate? The frankly partisan speaker has the advantages of consistent enthusiasm. He can plead and preach. He can be a "leader." He can make use of the comforting illusion that difficult questions have simple answers. His words have the natural speed and power of controversy. It is an easier role to play.

The educator responsible for managing a forum program can make use of advocates, recognizing that they will appeal to his audience. He can give his hearers balance by offering them the choice of watching gladiators of ideas in a give-and-take battle, or one after another at discreet intervals. Probably all forum programs need to make frequent use of these exciting conflicts.

The earnest, serious people who seek enlightenment, however, are numerous in any population. They need intellectual bread as well as intellectual circuses. For them a third sort of forum teacher is needed, one who neither conceals nor advocates his own opinions. He maintains his own critical attitude and scrupulously makes the best case he can for the opinions he rejects before he presents his reasons for rejecting them. He offers authoritative information and does not shirk the uncomfortable complexities, qualifications, and contradictions in which every important question is enmeshed. He tries to be a guide rather than a driver, and he has not failed if in the final result his hearers take him at his word and disagree with him.

Of this kind of forum teacher there is a great dearth because such discussion of exciting questions is extraordinarily difficult. It is also unpopular unless done with great skill and real moral, as well as intellectual, authority. The manager of a forum program will be handicapped in offering this fare to his clientele by the lack of available teachers. But in the future, as adult education becomes more professional, there will doubtless be more teachers fitted by training and temperament for interpretation, and the scope and usefulness of the forum will be greatly increased.

RADIO

It is commonly asserted and evidently believed that radio broadcasting is to be an important factor in adult education, but very little study has been made of the way in which it may be used. Too much time has been wasted in quarreling with the commercial broadcasters or in trying to get legal control of a fixed portion of the radio facilities. Not enough thought has been given to adapting educational material to broadcasting techniques. If European countries, particularly Great Britain, are more successful in broadcasting education than is the United States, it seems due more to the care with which their educational material is prepared and put on the air than to the fact that the government controls the programs.

Much of what has been said about lectures is applicable also to radio broadcasting. Something may be said in addition. In the first place, the habit of radio listening leads to a more or less indiscriminate turning of the dial at convenient times. Whatever would teach radio listeners to discriminate would mark a first step in making real use of the air as an educational medium.

It should be possible to inject a good many educational elements, particularly aesthetic ones, such as music and drama of first-rate quality, into programs which people accept as mere entertainment. Programs of definitely better quality for those already trained to appreciate them are no doubt of great importance, and provision must somehow be made for them, if not by commercial sponsors then by subsidy. But of even greater importance is the slow rise of public taste which comes from unexpected exposure to better things. As was indicated in connection with liberal studies, a higher general appreciation of art may be brought about more quickly by hanging good pictures in grocery stores and shop windows than by urging people to put themselves through the concentrated experience of an art museum. So it may be more effective for this purpose to scatter good music and drama, sound thought and lively discussion throughout the popular programs than to nurture only the highly specialized programs for the elite. The sensible educator will doubtless try to do both.

The radio is not, under ordinary circumstances, the best means of conveying information. Broadcasting is rather a stimulus to further thinking and reading. In this, the radio broadcaster is more a discussion leader than a lecturer, and his method should take the difference into account.

Since both lectures and discussion meetings should be followed by study and further consideration of opinions aired, and are not of fullest value unless they are so followed, we find that radio broadcasting is of little value unless it induces other activity. Any use of these three methods, the lecture, the discussion, or the broadcast, which leads to complacency or the satisfaction of a trivial interest is, of course, a misuse. The danger is in taking them as ends in themselves. They are, all three, dialectic methods of arousing minds and of encouraging the curiosity which seeks further knowledge and clearer thought.

We may settle into conventional ways of using radio broadcasting before we have discovered its full possibilities. Lectures have been studied since the days of the sophists and rhetoricians, and the dialectic of conversation for almost as long a time, and yet no one would say that we know enough about them to use them most wisely in our current ways of thinking and doing. The radio is so new that we are still amusing ourselves with its mechanical marvelousness. Several research organizations are trying to understand its possibilities. If through them an experimental attitude can be maintained for a sufficiently long time, there is hope that the techniques will not become ossified too fast and that discoveries will go on.

LABORATORY AND STUDIO WORK

When a mature student undertakes some educational experience which involves the use of his hands, he is at a greater disadvantage as compared with the child than in purely mental exercise. Manipulative skills, whether for creative expression or laboratory investigation, involve necessarily the hand and the eye. These are physiological, and the hardiest optimist has never maintained that the hand, the eye, and the nerves do not deteriorate with age. Simple manipulative techniques can doubtless be acquired by adults for industrial or recreational purposes. New industrial skills can be attained, provided they are not too complex or delicate. All the uses of manipulative experiences on the adult level, however, must take physiology into account.

It is doubtful if laboratory work, therefore, can ever play as illuminating a part in the study of science for an adult as it unquestionably can in such study by a youthful person. The limitations need not deter the ambitious; they are only guides for the teacher, the curriculum maker, and the planner of volunteer programs. No doubt the amateur student of astronomy is happy to look through a telescope and one who has been reading biology starts his own quest into the wonders of the microscopic world. He may even try to see things which have never been seen before. But on the scientific side, insofar as we are dealing with the laboratory rather than the studio, he is better equipped in his mature years for appreciation than for creative activity. His experience may be adapted to that limitation.

When one enters the studio, however, every consideration of method is different. Whereas, in the laboratory, one may be seeking only such knowledge of the technological side of science as will make his reading more easily understood; in the studio one is seeking a more intimate acquaintance with some art not only for appreciation but for self-expression. The studio experiences of adults appear to be most educational in their results when they are least formally educational in their atmosphere. That is to say, men and women approach the arts best when their play instinct is appealed to and given free rein. They discover problems for themselves if they undertake to express an ideal or to make something, and they accept more formal teaching in answer to these problems when once they have discovered them in that

way. Courses in design come most acceptably to those
adults who have first tried to draw or to paint. The
studio experience precedes the theoretical consideration.
Similarly, courses in harmony and in the history of
music are usually most interesting to those who have
tried to play or sing.

There appears to be here a somewhat paradoxical
reversal in order between the use of the laboratory or
manipulative techniques in the teaching of science and
the participatory exercise in teaching the arts. The difference depends upon the creative appeal of the arts, which
is lacking in the scientific work of the laboratory except
to those who have sufficient training and sufficient knowledge to attempt very delicate manipulation. A laboratory is best used to give concrete knowledge of methods
to the adult student who from his reading about science
has become interested in the way by which scientific
facts may be investigated. Knowledge of music, on the
other hand, comes after the attempts to express oneself
in music. Knowledge of art as a subject similarly suc-
ceeds the studio experience.

This is not to say, of course, that such an order is
always followed or always should be. Here, again, we are
making an attempt only to put down what seem to be at
present the best possible conclusions as to method. It
may be said in contradiction that any experience with
materials is refreshing to most people. Particularly, an
adult who has not been a worker in intellectual things
all his life finds reading and the extended abstractness
of printed discourse extremely wearisome. To touch
something, to handle an instrument or a tool, to get even
a discouraging knowledge of the refractoriness of material, or to see a fine craftsman at work in the intimate
surroundings of his shop is an experience of stimulating
value.

TEACHING BY CORRESPONDENCE

The fundamental methods of teaching adults can be applied to correspondence instruction, with recognition of the fact that teacher and pupil are not actually confronted. Much of what is said in another place regarding visual materials is of special importance to correspondence instruction. The larger commercial schools and university-extension divisions have made good use of all the known devices for producing easily comprehended reading material.

A good correspondence course in any subject must be put together with certain provisions which will make it possible for the student to get what he is after. They may be summarized as follows:

General directions for a course must be complete and clear. Authors preparing such material are much more likely to err in the direction of brevity and to take too much for granted than they are to explain at too great length. The student cannot be left in any possible doubt of what he is trying to do and why he is doing it. Here the general principle of dividing work into short units with quite easily seen and definite goals which leave impressions of rewarded effort in the student's mind is especially important.

In general instructions for a correspondence course it is only fair that the student should be able to estimate the length of time he will need to complete it, considering his own powers and the amount of energy he has available.

As the student progresses, he must be provided with devices for testing his learning and checking his mistakes against comprehensible standards.

Most correspondence students begin with a high potential interest in what they are about to do, but writing lessons in the loneliness of one's own home without anything more than a long-awaited letter to praise or blame is at best a wearisome business. Every device that can make a course of study interesting, flexible, evidently up-to-date in its information, and no more laborious than it needs to be will be so much gained. Since text and illustrations are the means of communication, the probable vocabulary and concept range of the student must be taken very carefully into account. New words and new ideas must be explicitly defined. Illustrations must be either so simple and clear that they can be interpreted by anyone, or given full explanation in the text.

General instructions and special advice on any particular unit should not rob the student of his own initiative, and he should not feel that a teacher is at his elbow even in the written word. His own initiative is one of the things which the course is undertaking to bring out. This leads to further emphasis of the necessity for having devices for self-testing and providing that the student should be required to send back to his teacher only such materials as are necessary to give measurable evidence of his accomplishment.

SELF-DIRECTED STUDY

Ultimately the goal of all adult education is the independent pursuit of learning. But, desirable as the constant growth of independence may be, it still remains that some kinds of learning will always have to be done in the society of fellow students. Some kinds of learning will always depend upon the guidance of a leader or teacher.

Really independent study can scarcely be directed by any "method" except the one invented by the student out of his own experience. The world has always been full of books telling people how to think, but most of us continue to think in our own ways. "One man cannot tell another how to think; he can simply tell the other how he thinks himself." [1]

There are few masters of any subject, however, who cannot learn from others; and in its advanced phases, self-directed education, the intellectual recreation of the mature person, faces two unpleasant extremes. On the one hand is the danger of isolation, and on the other, the danger of prolonged subservience. By too much independence, one may cut himself off from the stream of general knowledge, a mistake the professional student seldom makes. In the humility of great knowledge, the professional student scarcely ever finds it possible to do his thinking alone; he wants to know what all other workers in the field are discovering, if for no better reason than to save himself from duplicating the labors of others and searching out the facts already known. The danger of too-long-continued subservience to the guidance of a teacher is that one may never take on the authority of a mastery that has been earned and the responsibility which it implies. Such limits to endeavor lie far ahead of the ordinary adult student. They are real, however, in the intellectual life, and any student starting out upon the long journey may expect to meet new problems of association and detachment as he goes.

QUESTIONS FOR DISCUSSION

1. Discuss the use of classwork and of each of the special methods in relation to each of the five functions.

[1] Mortimer J. Adler, *Dialectic*, Harcourt, Brace and Company, 1927, p. 108.

2. What do you consider the most important qualities in a classroom lecturer? In a popular lecturer? Explain any differences.

3. Prepare a half-hour lecture for a popular audience on any subject with which you are familiar. Submit both outline and text.

4. Make a list of issues which your class could discuss, testing them by the following standard:
   a. Is each issue clearly one that can be settled only as a matter of opinion?
   b. Do the members of the class have the facts necessary for forming opinions?
   c. Is discussion of these issues likely to lead to modification or clarification of opinion?
   (These issues can be used in experimental groups).

5. If a conclusion must be based on a partial knowledge of the facts involved in the issue, because full knowledge is impossible, can the evidence as to the inaccessible facts be discussed?

6. Describe a discussion in which you have recently taken part. Was there a leader by appointment or as an actual result of personalities and circumstances? Was the leader useful or not? Why? What did the members of the group expect to get out of it? If they were not satisfied, explain why. Were any flaws in the discussion due to faulty framing of the issue?

7. What radio programs not definitely educational in intent do you consider educational in effect?

8. Who is your preferred radio news commentator? Why? Do you prefer music with comment or with-

out? Why? Does radio drama give you the same
emotional stimulus that you find in a theater or a
cinema?

9. Discuss any experience you have ever had with craftwork. What did you get out of it? Did any childhood
training in art or craftwork affect your adult interests? Has any attempt at artistic achievement
changed your appreciation of a master's performance?

10. Prepare a lesson in some subject you have taught to
be sent to a correspondence student. Discuss the reasons for the arrangement of material and for the instructions given.

READING REFERENCES

BITTNER and MALLORY, *University Teaching by Mail*, The
Macmillan Company, 1933.

FANSLER, THOMAS, *Discussion Methods for Adult Education
Groups*, American Association for Adult Education,
1934.

HOLLINGWORTH, H. L., *The Psychology of the Audience*,
American Book Company, 1935.

INSTITUTE FOR EDUCATION BY RADIO, *Yearbook*, Ohio State
University Press, 1930–1935.

LURIE, H. L., *The Challenge of the Forum*, Richard G.
Badger and Company, 1930.

STUDEBAKER, John W., *The American Way*, McGraw-Hill
Book Company, Chap. IV.

TYSON, LEVERING, *Education Tunes In*, American Association for Adult Education, 1930.

TYSON, LEVERING, ed., *Radio in Education* (Proceedings
of National Advisory Council on Radio in Education), University of Chicago Press, 1931–1935.

Chapter Eight

MATERIALS

VERY FEW materials have been formally and directly prepared for adult-education purposes. This is no doubt a handicap for classroom work, but in the widespread informal types of adult learning, leaders and students have relied with considerable success upon the whole range of cultural accumulation. For our purpose, materials may be described as Visual, Auditory, and Manipulative.

Visual. The printed word is still the most widely useful instrument for reaching and informing the adult population. Books, pamphlets, magazines, and newspapers are scattered everywhere. Although, as will be shown in discussing the public library, many people in the United States are not yet able to get books from public collections, it is still true that one can reach a wider audience through print than in any other way. The radio, which is auditory, may in time supplant the printed word. But that time has not yet come. Other visual materials are moving pictures (both visual and auditory), pictures and graphs, and the collections of objects in galleries and museums.

Auditory. Lectures have reached thousands in and out of scholastic classes, and the radio is reaching millions. Music and drama can be heard in concert halls or theaters, over the air, and from phonograph recordings.

Manipulative. Laboratory and studio experience has

been discussed under the heading of method. The drama is, for those who listen to it, an auditory experience, but for those who participate in its production the drama is properly classed as manipulative, that is, as an experience of physical action. Its greatest educational effect comes from participation. In music, also, there is more importance in production than in passive listening. Other combinations of auditory and physical action in learning may be found in the "nature walk" or the museum visit, in which examining objects is accompanied by a lecture.

For sound methodological reasons, it is of great importance that leaders in adult education should undertake to establish as much activity in their programs as is possible. The tendency will naturally be for adults to neglect those principles of learning which have become commonly accepted practice in teaching children. The youthful personality is most influenced by educational experiences which involve doing. Possibly in a lesser degree but still significantly, the same thing is true of the mature person. Participation in music, the dance, or the drama is something more than a way of acquiring an appreciation of fine performances by gifted stars. It is more than training for self-expression; it *is* self-expression.

FUNCTIONAL USES OF MATERIALS

Remedial. The chief remedial purpose is to teach men and women to read and write, particularly to read. Visual material is of primary usefulness. Books are the obvious resource, but pictures and some graphic representations of facts may be a more direct road to understanding than the unfamiliar printed words.

In the field of remedial education, there is probably a larger supply of available visual materials specially pre-

pared than in any other branch of adult work. Some of
it is adequate. A number of adaptations of great books
have been made for people of little reading experience,
and studies have been carried out as to the best method
of teaching reading to the student who has mature experience and normal intelligence, but no acquaintance
with printed symbols. Further psychological studies on
this point are now under way in several laboratories
and may be expected to yield fruitful results in the near
future.

As has been said before, however, remedial adult education fails in making the most of its chance unless the
attempt to learn reading and writing leads to a desire
for other types of learning. And even for the awakening of the mind and the strengthening of the learning
impulse, other materials than simple reading texts are
helpful. Music and the drama may be used, not only in
citizenship practice but also in elementary reading classes
to maintain self-respect and interest among the students.
Many students of no great aptitude for symbols and
abstractions are gifted in music or acting or the dance.
They may also be helped with moving pictures and may
be taught to listen more intelligently to the radio. Radio
listening groups can sometimes be organized where receiving sets are available. The radio and the cinema are
most useful to stimulate the student's desire to learn.
Both may be used constantly to point out that there are
many things on land and sea which cannot be understood unless one has the instruments of learning.

Books are still the fundamental material, and good
ones are not plentiful. Writing primers for people who
have not learned to read is a much more difficult task
than at first appears. The obstacles to adult learning,
emotional and intellectual, are in the way. The additional difficulty in the preparation of reading material

for beginners centers largely about the fact that the adult who is learning to read is actually learning a new set of symbols, visual instead of auditory. He can scarcely get much profit and is not likely to be interested in learning to read out of a child's primer. The concepts are not those with which he moves familiarly; he has outgrown them. Even the vocabulary, although simple, is not his vocabulary. The restricted vocabulary of a child in the normal school process and the restricted vocabulary of an adult who has not gone through school but has lived for twenty or thirty or forty years in normal daily life are not identical, nor even necessarily similar. The vocabularies are not the same, and the words which the child knows and uses cannot express the concepts that are of interest to the adult.

This makes necessary the first step, that special texts shall be written which undertake to put into simple terms the things in which mature people can find some interest in order that their learning motives may be sustained. Textbooks of this sort are scarce. The most useful reading now available is doubtless to be found in those rewritten classics in which the sweep and emotional current of the narrative carry the reader along in spite of occasional difficulties.

An adult can scarcely be expected to be able to read much with profit, however, until he can understand expository prose, explanation, and argument. Here very subtle difficulties lie in wait to trap the unwary teacher. It is not enough to know that a mature man can understand words when spoken and to point out to him that the same words are represented by a set of visual symbols on a sheet of paper. He has not learned to think in visual symbols. There is no reason for supposing that an illiterate has necessarily been inactive mentally, but his mental life has been built up by the use of sounds and direct, not symbolic, sights. His methods of thinking are different from those of the person who has been familiar with letters from childhood.

The extraordinary differences between certain peasant levels in the populations of Europe and the cultivated citizens of the same countries have often been pointed out. It is safe to say that one of the chief elements in this profound psychological difference lies in the fact that the peasants are not familiar with reading. Words are sounds to them, not sounds and printed signs both. Their use of a concept is often different from the use made by those who are associating that concept with the printed word. The same thing is true of large sections of the Negro population of the South and of the Mexican population of the Southwest in the United States. This is more easily understood by anyone who has learned stenography at a mature age and can analyze his own experience.

The teacher of an adult class in reading would do well to go upon the theory that his students are learning what amounts almost to a new language and not merely a new way of expressing a language that has long been familiar. Materials for these classes are difficult to produce, and much more psychological study and experiment is needed before sure standards can be established.

Occupational. For strictly occupational training, manipulative techniques are probably best. In this field, to learn to do by doing is the dominant principle. Lectures and texts, particularly if the lectures are well illustrated by demonstration, and if the texts follow the devices worked out by the correspondence schools for making things plain in diagram, will always be substantially helpful. But doing the thing to be learned, under the watchful eye and the helpful criticism of the instructor, is most satisfactory.

Relational. For educating men and women in wiser treatment of one another and in the adjustment of personal relationships, lectures, discussions, and books are the natural means. Parent education would include also the observation of nursery schools, and even laboratory demonstration. It may be suggested, however, that a very large part of what is learned in the adjustments among people, aside from what is acquired from the example of parents, teachers, and friends, comes from aesthetic experiences that stir the imagination and enrich the emotional life. In this branch of adult education particularly, the ideal effectively embodied for the student's emulation is the dominant factor in his learning. The general improvement of taste must inevitably lead human beings to treat one another with more forbearance and understanding. The great poets, novelists, and dramatists of the world have done more to change the emotions than textbooks or analytic treatises seem likely to do. The leader in this field may make use of all the world's art and literature; and in helping to raise public taste in regard to the radio, the moving picture, the theater, and even in simpler forms of recreation, he is making a contribution to this fundamental purpose.

Liberal. Since the distinctive characteristic of liberal education is doing things for their own sake, the materials are as broad as life itself. The obvious materials have already been listed. But in addition to these, all the forms of social contact may be used for their liberalizing effect, as well as travel, the investigation of one's environment, and anything that will open up the mind and the imagination. The materials for liberal adult education are the accumulations of civilization. And although reading books, listening to lectures, and enjoying the various arts are usually the most accessible means of satisfying the need for liberal experience, nothing that has the desired stimulating effect should be ruled out because it was not created for the purpose.

In the older meaning of the term, a liberal education necessarily included an acquaintance with the past. Indeed, it is still true and always will be that very little of the present or of the future can be understood unless the past is understood. The records of the past are the natural source of most of our materials because here one follows the humanist's ideal, to be acquainted with the best that has been thought and done in the world. But the contemporary has a liberalizing influence as well as a pragmatic importance, and an educated man is not homeless in his own time.

Political. No citizen in any modern country can escape political education. In a democracy he is sought after for his vote. And modern dictatorships are characterized by the fact that they appeal to mass opinion even more assiduously than parties do in the self-governing nations.[1] All the engines of propaganda bear down upon the mature mind with political suggestions and appeals. It is our belief that the primary purpose of adult education is to arouse in the mature mind a rational skepticism, not to paralyze or even unduly to delay action, but to equip the citizen with intelligent knowledge which will make his action effective for his own purposes. This touches upon the question discussed under the heading of the political function and sums up the special problem of material that will enable the average person to understand the controversial questions of his own day.

READABLE BOOKS

The most serious lack of materials for adult education at the present time is not in formal books written for the

[1] Cf. Guy S. Ford, *Dictatorships in the Modern World*, University of Minnesota Press, 1935, *passim.*

specific purpose, but in general literature. There are not
enough readable books. There are not enough books
that are simple, lucid, inexpensive, and illuminating on
current public questions, on the arts, the sciences, and
the various concerns of mankind.[1] Librarians in touch
with the reading needs of the people have been asking
for such books fruitlessly for almost a generation. Forum
leaders find themselves balked in developing the study
which naturally would follow upon their meetings, because the reference materials available are too expensive
or too difficult for the average reader. There are, to be
sure, some newspaper and magazine writers who can
discuss current problems or other matters of general interest in a way that will appeal to the average person
and in terms that someone not an expert can understand.
But many such articles and newspaper stories are un-
trustworthy. The political material is tendentious, the
scientific material is careless of facts and qualifications,
and too often books on serious subjects meant to be
popular succeed only in being patronizing.

The need for simple, beginners' books in a wide variety
of subjects, written to catch the attention of a mature
person and to win his respectful and interested response,
is not an invention of the educators. The testimony of
the librarians proves its reality. It is inarticulate, however, since the people for whom such books should be
written are mostly unaccustomed to reading any kind of
books. One or two rebuffs from an unintelligible tome is
enough to discourage them. They want to know and to
understand, but their experiments have not persuaded

[1] If there is an exception to this, it is in the field of religion. The adult
Bible classes of the country are well supplied with reading. The annual
mission study texts of the Protestant churches and some of the periodical publications of the Roman Catholic Church are simple, straightforward, and are read by thousands who would find anything more
abstruse or "literary" too difficult for them.

them that they can ever get what they want out of
printed materials.

The truth is that the lack of such primers of knowledge
and of simple discussions of current affairs is due more to
the difficulty of producing them than to anything else.
Studies have only recently been begun on the problem of
"readability." We still live in the shadow of a time when
reading books was a privilege reserved for scholars and
the aristocracy. There are still pundits who say that
anyone who cannot read the books now being written
is not worth bothering about. There are others, also,
and these critics are much more worth attention, who
say that most subjects worth considering cannot be discussed in terms simple enough to be understood by people
who have not had a lengthy educational training. This
may be true, but we may be allowed to doubt it.

Extensive experiments will have to be carried out in
simplification and in the production of readable texts, as
well as experiments in their distribution and possible
sale, before all phases of the problem will be understood
and long before any easy solution can be found. It will
also be necessary to study the continuing effects of the
bad training in reading that most of our adult population suffered in elementary classes. The use of graphs
and diagrams, in which many people have faith, but
about whose effect we know very little, will also have
to be thoroughly investigated. And after all possible
information is put together, it may take years of expensive pioneering before the books themselves can be
put into the hands of their proper users.

Experimenters are trying to decide whether such primers should be written by people who are masters of the
subjects involved and then edited for a special public
by an expert in "readability," or written by people
trained both in techniques of presentation and in sub-

ject matter. They are trying to separate mere structural elements from difficulties that lie in concepts and in distribution of ideas. They are trying to find out what format and physical presentation are most appealing. They want to know how much of the dramatic and the emotional may be injected into a serious essay without misinforming the reader.

It should be understood, however, that this matter of more simple books on a great many different subjects is not only a question of reaching a special group of potential readers. Every person, no matter how well informed, is a beginner in many subjects and would be glad to have a simple, lucid introduction to any one of those subjects whenever his attention happens to be turned to it. The mind of each one of us works on different levels in different matters. We may want only the latest and most intricate of treatises on astronomy, but be woefully ignorant of politics. We may know a lot about music but not much about chemistry. The problem is to produce a book in each field (and the fields are innumerable) which will be not only for the "uninformed" reader but for all readers uninformed in that subject. The public for such books is a vast and complex one, and we all help to make it up.

In the special field of public affairs, however, there is a more urgent and direct demand for comprehensible, trustworthy accounts and interpretations of the facts. The average citizen does not know the sources of information, and if he is offered pertinent facts it is almost impossible for him to put them together in their proper meaning. Since democratic government is government by public opinion, the alert citizen is naturally suspicious of whatever comes to him from official sources. Still less can he trust the propaganda of special-interest groups and party publicity. No one has as yet worked out any scheme of publication under public or private subsidy, or in the hands of commercial publishers, that would altogether meet the demand for a completely disinterested source of information. In the meantime, a great many readers would be willing to support those writers and publishers whom they felt they could reasonably trust. The responsibility of the adult-education leader in this matter is clear. He has not only to further experiments and efforts in this direction to the utmost, but also to act as a guide in the general reading of all who turn to him for help.

He can do this best if he realizes in the beginning that there are millions of people in America who are quite eager to listen to talks on subjects about which they are unlikely to read. It is not only that they are unaccustomed to reading on serious questions. There are other difficulties. Many of these people, and every forum leader knows them, have never learned how to judge the validity of what is offered on the printed page. When they hear a speaker, they can make a rough calculation of his honesty by looking at him and studying him as a human being. They feel that they can depend on their own judgment in a face-to-face encounter, and make a shrewd guess as to the trustworthiness and sincerity of the speaker's remarks. When they get into the less familiar world of the printed word, and the tangible personality of the speaker is withdrawn, they are more or less consciously aware of the fact that they are at a writer's mercy. The trained and sophisticated person may be less at the mercy of a writer than of a speaker. Be that as it may, the average American citizen of mature years is more willing to trust his own judgment of a speaker than of a printed document. There are millions, of course, who are innocently responsive to appeals, whether in print or in speech, and ready to be swayed in any direction the winds may blow. But there are other millions who are uneasy in the knowledge of their own helplessness. It is for them especially that a new kind of book on public problems must be written, a book which will convey the straightforward honesty of a good forum lecturer, that will give in terms that any intelligent man can understand both conclusions and the basis for conclusions, that will answer the questions which the man in the street wants to have answered, that will meet him where he is and help him to get farther down the road he wants to travel.

QUESTIONS FOR DISCUSSION

1. Which do you consider most effective, plain text? text with illustrations? graphs? text with graphs? Can you support your opinion with any evidence?

2. Read a portion of one of the simplified versions of a literary classic. What has been lost? What retained? What effect would this reading have on the taste of the adult elementary student?

3. What materials (visual, auditory, manipulative) have you used in any teaching of children you have done? Which would you include in teaching the same subject to adults? How modified?

4. To what extent should materials for adult education be prepared so as to be effective without the intervention of a teacher? To what extent is this possible?

5. Discuss the educational uses of the drama and the dance, choral singing and orchestra playing. Do you distinguish between educational and recreational uses?

READING REFERENCES

GRAY and LEARY, *What Makes a Book Readable*, Chicago University Press, 1935.

GRAY and MONROE, *Reading Interests and Habits of Adults*, The Macmillan Company, 1929.

ROBINSON, JAMES HARVEY, *The Humanizing of Knowledge*, George H. Doran and Company, 1926.

WAPLES and TYLER, *What People Want to Read About*, Chicago University Press, 1931.

Chapter Nine

ORGANIZATION AND PROMOTION

THE WORK of the past has been carried on in all kinds of places, some of them rich in traditions, like the Great Hall of Cooper Union, some mere makeshifts, like the untenanted barns that have been transformed into art schools or little theaters. Management has usually been "committee work," and promotion nothing more than pooled enthusiasm. For the sake of vitality and sincerity, we may hope that these informal methods of organizing may continue wherever they will suffice. But the superintendent of a city's schools, or the director of a widely scattered net of university-extension centers, or any other official who deals with more systematic work must attend to the planning and details of administration. Adults who study under public auspices are not so ready to overlook the prosaic matters of "efficiency."

The general techniques for administration of plant and equipment have been worked out for public schools as thoroughly as for any American institution. A person responsible for managing the physical equipment of an adult-education agency would do well to acquire some of the knowledge expected of a trained school superintendent. This is true even if he is administering the night classes of a Y.M.C.A. or an even less formal gathering of people. For the person who directs the night activities of the public-school system, principles of administration are not readily distinguishable from those which govern the work of a day-school executive. If there are any differences, they are no doubt covered in the lengthy explanation of all the detailed phases of night-school management given in such a book as *Adult Education: The Evening Industrial School*, by Prosser and Bass.

Many people responsible for adult programs, however, are not in any sense trained managers. This might be a much better world if one could always be sure that common sense and a reasonable thoughtfulness would enable these program managers to do, without special professional knowledge, all the things that have to be done. There are philosophers of education who think that a director's time is wasted if given to consideration of the physical surroundings in which the educative process is expected to go on. And, of course, a student with a bright vision of what he hopes to accomplish and a burning desire to make the best of his own powers can put up with bad light, bad air, bad seating, and all the other afflictions which bad management may put upon him. It is not only more humane but also more intelligent to realize, however, that the person who pursues mental advancement in his free time has generally completed a hard day's work before he undertakes this added task. He is already past the peak of his best effort. He has fatigue to fight against, even if every other circumstance is in his favor. Great teaching can doubtless be done in foul and dingy places, but great teaching is rare in any kind of place; and the student does not enjoy learning the more because he is uncomfortable. It is not necessary to discuss at length the fairly simple but fundamentally important matters of being a good host to a group of adult learners. But it is pertinent to insist that kindly hospitality and a decent concern for the comfort of others are proper things for an administrator to show and to be alert to teach.

PROMOTION

It is part of our basic theory of adult education that men and women take part in it because of their own felt needs. Promotion is necessary, nevertheless. It is necessary because continued learning is not yet established as a natural way of spending leisure time. In accordance with our folkways, young people consider themselves students; their elders think of themselves as past the learning stage. Promotion can inform them of further chances for learning. It can tell them of the offerings of helpful intellectual or recreational activities that are being enjoyed by adults like themselves.

Promotion and publicity are necessary even in the advancement of a self-directed activity, because freedom of choice is as much limited by ignorance as by anything else. No one can choose to do something which he has never heard of doing. It is nonsense to say that people do not wish to do things which they have never been offered a chance to do. Promotion in adult education is essentially an invitation to inspect a program.

It is important to note that there are fundamental differences between what is possible in publicity for an educational enterprise and those devices and appeals which make up the highly developed commercial publicity under whose pressure we all live. In commercial publicity, two things are nearly always present. First, there is an appeal by means of prestige; second, there is an appeal to our faith in fairy tales. We are supposed to prefer certain cigarettes, automobiles, tooth pastes, or what not, because people of social importance prefer them—or are willing for a generous subsidy to say in public that they prefer them. This is based partly on downright snobbishness, partly on the well-established psychological principle that we are much more hospitable toward ideas if they come from people whom we admire.

And the other principle is not often absent even if not explicitly declared. Much advertising is in effect a promise that, if we will surrender a small amount of cash, we can be miraculously endowed with new strength, power, or beauty, or miraculously saved from the consequences of some common folly. We can drink too much and still have no headache if we buy the right powders. Nature may have made us ugly, but if we will buy the right lotion we can cure all that. The important element in this appeal to gullibility is that it does not require any effort or contribution from the consumer except a small part of his income.

The promotion of adult education can in some degree make use of the first principle, but it is handicapped by the advertisement-reading habits of the people created by the second principle. Adult education acquires a certain prestige when it is pointed out that men of the highest professional training usually continue their studies throughout professional life, and that there is a true but indefinite relation between knowledge and success. The prestige appeal can be used by acquainting still larger groups of people with the fact that large groups are already deeply interested.

But adult education can promise no miracles. There have, of course, been advocates of the movement who have offered it as a cure-all for present evils. A sound and continuing program of promotion could scarcely be based on any such optimism. It will always be difficult to devise publicity for adult education if the truth is told. The best any educational agency can do is to offer a chance to work. The return to any student will be largely in proportion to the effort the student exerts. Promotion can promise rewards for that effort more substantial and more worth while than most of the things that are sold by advertising. But commercial advertising methods are dangerous models to follow.

The chief device in educational publicity will probably always be to attract new learners by keeping the general public well informed of what present learners are doing. That can be done in newspapers, and by posters and circulars distributed wherever they may attract attention.

States, counties, cities, and less well-defined regions have experimented with the promotion of adult education by the organization of councils. Various institutions and persons have joined together to pool information and gain by co-operation. These bodies have had varied programs in addition to the one essential purpose of promoting the movement, and some have persisted for a number of years. They have practically all been helped by subsidies from foundations or from public-spirited citizens, and no way has yet been found to carry on their work without some kind of philanthropic financial support. Some have lecture bureaus or information bureaus which bring them revenue. But in their strictly promotional activity, they have little chance of being independent. Since agencies which actually do educational work are in practically all cases supported by endowments or tax money, it is not likely that one which exists for the purpose of merely promoting an educational interest can do without some help.

There is a further difficulty in the fact that a council or organization for the promotion of the idea is most successful when it has induced other agencies to undertake a program rather than when it has carried on operations itself. This leads to a degree of anonymity, and it is in the nature of things that credit for success should come to the agency which has been induced by the council to act, rather than to the council which has supplied the encouragement. In other words, the better a common organization does its own job of promoting adult education in general, the more interest and support will accrue to various institutions with which it is dealing rather than to itself.

It is entirely possible that the general promotional problems of the future will be met by the activities of professional organizations made up of people interested in this field. The battles of public-school education in this country are fought by the professional groups of teachers and administrators who work in the public system. They supply leadership for the elements in each community that are aware of educational values. Adult education will continue, no doubt, to include both scholastic and non-scholastic leaders as well as many volunteer workers, and it is difficult to say what form professional organizations will take or how strong they may get to be. Their development, however, may be taken for granted.

DISCOVERING INTERESTS

It is easy to say that adult education is always a response to the felt need and declared purpose of a mature student, but the administrator who is promoting a program cannot safely rest in the belief that the adults of his community will come to him of their own accord and demand the things that will meet their desires. The problem is not so simple. It is complicated by the fact that people do not know what they are interested in, except in terms of what is available to them. As has been repeated before, ignorance is a limitation on freedom of choice. Communities often seem to be inert because they have insufficient stimulation and leadership. Even deeply felt desires are not likely to find articulate expression until those who feel them have been in some way assured that there is an agency interested in their plight. The intellectual appetite, like the appetite for food, is roused by the sight of viands prepared. The administrator is constantly making an adjustment between his present program and the marginal activities which he thinks might be welcomed by his clientele and which he can try out by suggestion.

The administrator who is beginning a new program is in a somewhat different position. He has the problem of determining what he will offer in the hope of getting the greatest possible initial response and being thus assured of a good start. His first recourse is to the programs of other communities not too different from his own. They show what other people have been interested in, and the suggestion to his own clientele that certain things have found support in other places may be in some degree an enticement.

A second thing that the founder of an adult-education program can do is to make a survey of the "interests" of his possible supporters. Interest-finders are of many kinds, and there are forms available for those who wish to follow established methods. The best sort of interest-finder is the one which suggests the greatest possible number of choices in the most attractive possible way. An interest-finder should be used with the understanding that people are not always the best reporters of their own permanent interests. Many things stand in the way of a frank and accurate description by any person of his own scale of values and attitudes. Some people, confronted with a check list, wish to seem more thoughtful or intellectual than they are. In other cases, quite ephemeral interests are over-emphasized unconsciously. Sometimes an exotic description will attract someone's momentary attention although the pursuit of the subject indicated would not hold that particular person for any length of time. These are handicaps in the way of discovering what people really want, but the attempt to do so has value in arousing a general interest in continuing education.

What people actually do, it cannot be too often said, does not establish what they are most deeply concerned about. What they want to do, what they are most interested in, must always be adjusted to the opportunities offered. Studies of the reading of people in places where large numbers of books are available have shown conclusively that if there is a book at hand which satisfies a third- or fourth-degree interest the reader will take it rather than make a journey to a not-distant place where a book on a subject which ranks number one in interest could be found.[1] This fact makes it possible for the administrator to adjust his program so that the highest number of genuine impulses may be met without attempting to create such a kaleidoscopic pattern as would represent the actual spread of all the declared interests of his public.

NATIONAL ORGANIZATION

One reason for taking 1926 as a turning point in the development of adult education in America is that in that year the American Association for Adult Education began its active work. It was founded by the Carnegie Corporation, and in ten years of existence it has been the channel through which large sums of money have been spent by the Corporation on experiments, demonstrations, and development. Other foundations have occasionally put funds at its disposal for special purposes.

[1] Harriet R. Forbes, "The Geography of Reading," *A. L. A. Bulletin*, August, 1935.

No attempt will be made here to give an account of the Association's various activities or an adequate description of its influence upon the making of policy and the growth of ideas. This has all been set forth in *Ten Years of Adult Education* by Morse A. Cartwright, the director.

A national society with an advisory committee including most of the leaders in the field, and backed by foundation funds, is in a position to contribute not only money but moral support to demonstrations and experiments. It can go much further in taking risks than public agencies are likely to go. It can subsidize costly research and break new ground. The American Association has done these things. Its quarterly Journal and its Handbook are essential documents. Books published directly and indirectly by the Association are numerous enough to attract attention in any bibliography on the subject.

In ten years the Carnegie Corporation has made grants in support of adult education amounting to nearly $3,000,000. Of this total, nearly $2,000,000 has gone into useful experiment. It would be difficult to imagine a phase of adult education that has not been touched and there are very few which have not been substantially advanced by this help. The only activity in the field from which the American Association has held aloof is the direct preparation of materials on controversial social and political questions. It has, however, advised in the granting of large sums of money to such institutions as the Des Moines Public Forums where public questions of controversial character were freely discussed. It has also helped in the investigation of techniques by which such materials can be prepared.

The adult-education movement during the last ten years has been not only aided but in some measure guided in policies by the American Association. Because it has been able to include in its council most of the leaders in various types of work, both public and private, volunteer and professional, the Association has expressed through its publications much of the best thinking that has gone on while policies were taking shape. The advice of the American Association, as expressed through the Journal, in the annual reports of the director, and in national annual conferences, is not guidance in the sense of direct professional regulation for which, of course, the Association has neither authority nor mandate. Nor does this advice determine practices, although the Association assembles and disseminates a good deal of practical information. The Association's greatest usefulness has been in maintaining a sound conception of the role played by adult education in social progress. Above all, the American Association has been effective in keeping the movement from becoming either doctrinaire or undemocratic. The official documents of the Association have expressed always a clear realization that adult education is most important in the growth of American culture because it is an agency for the creation and re-creation of genuine values, that it looks beyond the practical end of the moment, both social and individual, and builds for the future.

QUESTIONS FOR DISCUSSION

1. Make a critical report of the physical equipment and management of the institution in which you are now studying. Suggest remedies for any faults you find.
2. Study the advertising pages of a current periodical, and make a list of the motives to which the advertisements appeal. Could any of these be used as a basis for promoting educational activity?

3. What is the relation between education and worldly success?
4. Make a list of your own chief interests. Compare it with a list of your chief activities with the time allotted to each. If there are discrepancies, how do you explain them?
5. What are the differences between a trade association in business and a "council" of educational agencies?

READING REFERENCES

BRYSON, LYMAN, *A State Plan for Adult Education*, American Association for Adult Education, 1934.

HERRING, JOHN W., *Social Planning and Adult Education*, The Macmillan Company, 1933.

OZANNE, JACQUES, *Regional Surveys of Adult Education*, American Association for Adult Education, 1934.

PROSSER and BASS, *Adult Education: The Evening Industrial School*, D. Appleton-Century Co., 1930.

REEVES and GANDERS, *School Building Management*, Bureau of Publications, Teachers College, Columbia University, 1928.

STACY, W. H., *Integration of Adult Education*, Bureau of Publications, Teachers College, Columbia University, 1935.

Chapter Ten

AGENCIES IN ADULT EDUCATION:
THE PUBLIC SCHOOLS

THE NEXT section of this book comprises brief accounts of
some of the major agencies now working in the field of
adult education. These descriptions are not exhaustive.
For statistical information concerning any agency the
student may go to the *Handbook of Adult Education*, which
covers the field and is kept up to date. Special literature
on many of the agencies mentioned is available, con-
taining critical discussions of policies and achievements
which will be interesting to the patrons and the workers
in each branch. No general description can give a picture
of the local activities of every one, nor provide a student
with a guide to the resources available in his community.
A knowledge of the more common agencies working
over the country will, however, help him to know what
to expect. To the workers in adult education, professional
and volunteer, administrators, teachers, and leaders, it is
useful to have some knowledge of the extended brother-
hood of which they are members.

Adult education is not more free of institutional jeal-
ousies and conflicts than are other fields of public service.
The isolation in which many pioneers have worked has
given them the illusion that they are the sole inventors of
methods and the sole possessors of answers to the public
needs. This is to be expected in the beginning stages of

a developing movement. Co-operation and fruitful exchange of experience come from better understanding.

In order to understand the operations of typical agencies, every student should make at least one survey, either of an agency or of a community. The survey of an institution should include a comprehensive listing of all its program activities with an analysis of each in terms of the adult-education functions which it fulfills. A community may be studied in terms of its social, economic, and educational needs. To this pattern should be fitted an analyzed description of its resources, public and private, scholastic and nonscholastic, for meeting these needs.

THE PUBLIC SCHOOLS

The awakening of public-school officials to their responsibility in adult education has been one of the most striking changes of the last decade. In this awareness, school officials have been reflecting several influences. First, there has been the growing intellectual curiosity of the American people, aroused by distress and bewilderment. The rising level of educational experience and interest would have brought on the change in any case, but economic troubles hastened it. The public has done a characteristic thing in demanding that opportunity for lifelong learning be made available to all classes of people through public agencies. The only agency able to meet this demand on a large scale is the public-school system. An added influence which has increased the interest of public-school workers in the needs of mature men and women has been their own increased professional competence and better training, which have given them an understanding of the total task of education in relation to a whole community. They are themselves part of the public and help to make the general public opinion, and their own problems have made continued learning more and more necessary to them. A recent influence has been the intervention of the government, largely through the public schools.

Some functions of adult education have always been a major concern of the public system, particularly remedial work, Americanization, and occupational training for younger adults. Now the public schools are taking on liberal and political studies. Many educators of adults who have been deeply concerned with the movement feel that this public intervention will be harmful. For a hundred years, independent and volunteer organizations have carried the work forward. It is natural for the leaders of these free agencies to feel the danger of tightening formality and rigid control if professional administrators and classroom teachers are to take over the bulk of their work.

The danger is real. It would be unfair, however, to thousands of alert administrators and teachers to suppose that all imagination in education is outside the public system and that initiative can be shown only by volunteer groups. If the plainly seen danger is taken seriously enough, it may be avoided. In any case, adult education has a protection against rigidity and formalism which does not exist in secondary or elementary classes. If adult education is not satisfactory, the students do not come to school. There will doubtless always be a great many independent volunteer groups carrying on work after their own fashion and to their own ends. They will serve as a corrective for any unsatisfactory public work. They will experiment and invent more freely than public systems can do. They will stimulate and correct.

Whatever the effect, in the next decade a large part of the program will pass into the hands of professional school people. The trend toward public adult education is not likely to be reversed, and there is fundamentally no reason why it should be. But we have been insisting that grown men and women must be allowed to set their own educational goals. Public-school officials and teachers must learn a new attitude toward a new clientele. It may be said, of course, that the better schools do their best to fit practices to the needs and desires of young students; but, in any case, to a child one must necessarily say, "Here are phases of the culture of your people with which you will need to be acquainted if you are to support yourself and live as a citizen of the community in which you happened to be born." As has been pointed out, the adult is seeking not the patterns by which he is to live but is coming back to study either for the modification of these patterns if he hopes to swing a social change, or to alter his own situation in things as they are. He will choose for himself what he wants to learn.

The virtues, not the faults, of the trained administrator are likely to bring him to grief in dealing with older students. He is accustomed to prescribing courses of study. He has tried to make programs which will save the time of his teachers and the use of all the other resources such as materials and equipment and rooms. He has taken pride in keeping unit costs as low as possible. When he turns to the organization of adult classes and more informal groups, it would be quite natural for him to measure success in management by much the same standards. But we know, considering the nature of adult learning and the goals of adult effort in self-education, that standards of mechanical efficiency may defeat the purpose.

The public-school teacher as well as the administrator is likely to find difficulty in shifting over to the teaching of adults. Teachers well trained for elementary classroom work can very well turn, with some modifications in method, to the teaching of adults, but only if they have sufficient flexibility and intelligence. It is not the most flexible and teachable teachers who are likely to be given assignments to adult work in the ordinary school system. It is much more likely that members of the staff will be chosen because they have distinguished themselves by long and successful experience in the teaching of the immature. The characteristic experience of a lifetime, or even a large part of a lifetime, spent in the classroom with boys and girls is not the experience to give a person those attitudes that will make him most adaptable in teaching men and women.

On a functional basis, it is easy to see that there are more dangers in some areas than in others. Remedial education has been carried on almost entirely by the public schools. Taxpayers are quite convinced that it should be a public responsibility. It is not likely that any other agency could have accomplished as much. There will doubtless be expansion of this work in the future as more imagination is applied in the adult-education program. The economics and hygiene of the home will be added in time. Visiting teachers will carry enlightenment and health to underprivileged families.

In occupational training, the public-school administrators need make very little adjustment of their present activities except to acquire faith in the capacity of the grown person to take on new skills and aptitudes. Methods of training in occupations can be successfully transferred from younger to older students without much difficulty.

For these first two functions of adult education there is hope of getting further public support without strong opposition. Remedial work has been well supported if one takes into account the fact that places which are

badly in need of remedial programs are places where education is little understood and not generally believed in.

For occupational training, it may be somewhat less
easy to get public funds. It will be years, no doubt,
before the average American taxpayer realizes the fundamental economic fact that an unproductive citizen is a
loss not only to himself but to the community as a whole.
To put it in another way, a man who is improved in
earning capacity helps not only himself but everybody
else. That this should make it advisable on a cold cash
basis to enable everyone to increase his productiveness,
even at public cost if necessary, seems a logical conclusion. One may confidently predict that public-school
systems will eventually offer occupational training and
retraining to anyone of any age who asks it at any time.
This will not be generosity, it will be good business.

Education in personal relationships has been up to
now largely confined to the parent-education movement,
and this has had a strong alliance with the public schools.
The most vigorous and widespread support given to
parent education by any single agency has been that of
the Parent-Teacher Associations, and they are closely related to public schools in their thinking and dependent
upon public schools for their operation. For reasons that
have already been stated, it is not likely for many years
at least that parent education or any other relational
studies will be taken over entirely by the professional
teacher or leader. When one speaks of parent education
being brought more completely into public-school programs, he does not mean that lay leaders will disappear
and school teachers take their places. Objections to such
a change are obvious. But closer co-operation between
parents and teachers is possible, and closer co-operation
between schools and parent education groups will no
doubt be developed.

It seems less likely that the schools will assume large responsibility for liberal education than for any of the other functional types. This is not, of course, in any way certain. There may be a great development, in the not-too-distant future, of free and voluntary study under public-school auspices of all the things that interest and delight and bring recreation to men and women. The high schools have large resources for such work and the junior colleges, constantly growing in numbers and power, have in most cases enough in the way of people, books, and ideas to be the centers of liberal adult education for large communities. It was the opinion of Henry Suzzallo that the work of the junior college in adult education would be one of its chief claims to public support. In the field of liberal studies, however, predictions are of uncertain value. Much will depend on the kind of school systems, up through the junior colleges, that the parents of the future demand and endow.

What can public schools do in political education? To train a child in what we call "civics" and then turn him loose in the adult world without continuing guidance from some public agency which he has learned to trust seems educationally and politically shortsighted if not actually stupid. But can the schools give political training and constantly adequate new information to the voting people of their community? No confident answer can be given to this as yet, but it may be pointed out that there are examples of success which may well be studied by the fainthearted who see more dangers than chances of triumph.

The first difficulty in public political education is the fact that there is not now in existence in sufficient numbers a personnel capable of carrying on such work to spread a system of public forums or public classes in current affairs throughout the country. Forums which have been notably successful have been manned largely by people brought in from college faculties or by professional lecturers rather than by the staff of the local high schools or junior colleges. The desire to listen to wisdom from strangers may be only a passing phase, and one hopes that it will prove to be. If public political adult education is ever to be widespread and firmly rooted in American institutions, it will have to be carried on by local people for each community, by high-school teachers, lawyers, editors, clergymen, and others who have special capacity and access to information. For financial reasons it would be impossible to do otherwise. In time, one may expect that teachers of the social sciences and a good many other professional people will look forward to forum leading as a part of their life work and will train themselves adequately for the purpose.

The second great difficulty lies in the timidity of school boards' and of the groups that 'undertake to think for their fellow citizens. Many officials and many citizens of importance are not yet convinced that the people can be trusted with their own business. Happily, evidence is accumulating that citizens can be allowed to think for themselves and moreover that they will do so whether professional guardians of the public mind permit it or not. A courageous administrator is likely to succeed in establishing reasonable freedom if he is not afraid of those who criticize him.

These two difficulties are not unrelated. When the quality of forum leadership is improved, it will give greater confidence to the timid and the doubtful. When men who know in a reasonable degree all sides of current questions and can state fairly the conflicting opinions, men whose own opinions are respected because of their honesty and intelligence, are plentifully at work in public forums, this fear of free discussion will diminish.

If the dangers and difficulties mentioned are overcome, as they probably will be by the courage and intelligence of public-school leaders, one fundamental question will constantly recur and must be settled temporarily at least. If adult education is to be in large measure a public responsibility, who should pay for it? Debate on this question is usually between two extreme opinions. Some advanced advocates of continuing learning believe that a satisfactory public-school system will provide for every citizen a chance to learn whatever he wants to know whenever he wants to know it. Others say that this will impose a financial burden far beyond any possible funds available. Still others say that even if there were money to accomplish it, it would not be wise because older people should pay for their own education.

A study of history would indicate that the first opinion is most likely to prevail. In spite of all that has been urged against it and all that could be, a gradual expansion and enrichment of education at public expense goes on steadily and no man can estimate its final development. This will doubtless be made somewhat easier by the fact that the necessity for an education in the lower age groups is lessening because of the shift in the general age levels in the population, as has been explained elsewhere.

At the present time, the education of children has been seriously set back by economic loss and retrenchment. Complete programs of adult education entirely at public expense are scarcely possible in most communities now. They should, no doubt, be postponed.

There is an interim period, however, during which the responsibility of the public school can scarcely be met by standing by and waiting until sufficient money is in hand for a complete program at public expense. A compromise is called for. The responsibility of the public schools can be discharged even under present handicaps if the knowledge and experience of public-school administrators and the equipment of public-school teachers are put at the service of adult education, even if the students themselves have to pay a large part of the cost. It has already been pointed out that the demand for continued learning can never be measured until opportunities exist and are properly brought to the attention of potential users. This is an obvious duty of the public-school system.

Such studies as have been made of the effect upon adult students of charging fees would indicate that high fees—that is, payment anywhere near the full cost of the work—are a deterrent, and that very low fees have no particular effect, but that moderate fees, which give the adult learner a feeling of responsibility and of investment, tend to maintain classes and hold the student more earnestly to his labors. In this as in so many other cases, however, it should be stated that the nature of the work has a good deal to do with the attitude of the student, and that one who will pay gladly to learn a skill will probably resent having to pay a fee to participate in a discussion group on current affairs. Adjustments of the various parts of the program to the willingness of the public to pay as it goes should be the business of the understanding and skillful administrator.

Volunteer and independent adult-education enterprises must be supported either by those for whom they are working or by philanthropic funds. If adult education has the public values which we believe it has, it is a good investment for all the funds, public or philanthropic or from the pockets of users, that can be secured to support it. As far as adult education in the public schools is concerned, the financial burden will not be a very important handicap to progress. Few public-school systems are now ready to spend wisely more than 5 or 6 per cent of their ordinary budgets for this purpose, and most systems could make a worthy beginning with less.

Public administrators should seriously consider suggestions made by Thorndike and others to the effect that adult education may be a wise expenditure of public funds and of people's time even if the total number of hours spent in school is not to be increased. To put all public schooling in the years between six and sixteen, which is our present custom, rests upon nothing better than a superstition as far as actual learning power is concerned. The suggested alternative is to put children into practical work at an earlier age but to give them chances to continue their education in spare hours or at regular intervals for a much longer time.

To be sure, children are not capable of bearing their full share of the burden of self-support, and there are many social reasons for not putting them to work too young. This, however, may be exaggerated. Particularly, we may have overlooked the educative effects of certain kinds of work which young people could do. Any such suggestions usually meet with resistance because it is believed that they mean a denial of opportunities to the children who go early to work. Nothing of the sort is necessarily involved. If the total span of education allowed, following Thorndike's suggestion, is now normally about ten thousand hours in the classroom, it might be better to spread those ten thousand hours over the ages from six to twenty-six or even from eight to thirty than to concentrate them as we do now. To undertake any such adjustment would obviously involve rearrangement of our economic system and of our school system. But it is not beyond the range of imagination when one has grasped the fact that the best learning years are in the middle twenties. The public-school administrator of the future will probably feel as much responsibility for the intellectual life of the young people of his community in those middle twenties as he now does for all the child population of his school district of the age of nine or ten.

In any case, however, it appears to be a natural trend in the social order to enlarge constantly the total quantity of schooling considered a normal right for every human being. If the present ten thousand hours is increased to twelve or sixteen thousand hours in the future, some adjustment of adult life to free learning time will be necessary and will then be provided. First, however, it will be necessary to eradicate the traces of the illusion that learning beyond early youth is either a luxurious indulgence or a mere attempt to patch up a job that should have been done before. For this task the workers in the public schools have an opportunity and an inescapable responsibility.

QUESTIONS FOR DISCUSSION

1. By what social process have newer elements, such as music, art, and home economics, been added to the curricula of the public schools? Will this work out in similar ways in regard to adult activities?

2. Many teachers in secondary schools welcome the opportunity to teach adults in evening classes. Why do you think they take on this added work?

3. How much remedial adult education will public agencies carry on in the future?

4. How much of the whole adult-education activity of a community should the public schools expect ultimately to carry on? Does the size of the community make any difference?

5. What measurement devices can you suggest for judging the results of a community program in adult education?

READING REFERENCES

STATE OF CALIFORNIA, Department of Public Instruction, *Annual Reports*.

STATE OF DELAWARE, Department of Public Instruction, *Annual Reports*.

U. S. OFFICE OF EDUCATION, *Biennial Surveys of Education in the United States*.

STUDEBAKER, JOHN W., *The American Way*, McGraw-Hill Book Company, 1935.

Chapter Eleven

NATIONAL PUBLIC PROGRAMS

THE UNITED STATES government necessarily exerts an educational influence on all its citizens, especially since our democratic order involves all of us in public business. Control over schools, however, is centered in local units. Federal intervention in education, if we are to have it, must be by means of supporting grants which are usually matched by local funds. The very considerable federal intervention in education that we do have is mostly for the benefit of adults. The two chief federal programs are for the general betterment of rural life and for vocational training.

AGRICULTURAL EXTENSION

The Smith-Lever law, as it is generally known, was passed in 1914, "in order to aid in diffusing among the people of the United States useful and practical information on subjects relating to agriculture and home economics, and to encourage the application of the same." Experiment stations and agricultural colleges to encourage the technical development of professional agriculture have been in existence for a good many years. The systematic attempt to bring the federal government, as a teaching agency, to the support of the food- and fiber-producing industries was brought on by the obstreperous boll weevil. When this pest was ravaging the cotton fields of the South in 1904, the Department of Agriculture intervened, and direct help to farmers was established.

In more recent years, the Roosevelt administration has been active in farm economics through the Agricultural Adjustment Act and has widened the scope of extension. Between these major crises was the World War, which strained the food-producing resources of this country to the uttermost and aroused a loyal desire to meet the need.

Now, after more than twenty years' operation, the extension work of the United States Department of Agriculture in co-operation with states, with counties, with agricultural colleges, and with local farmers' organizations, is the largest single adult-education enterprise in the world. In 1935, it enlisted the services of 7,500 men and women on the payroll as county agents, home-economics agents, and in other technical positions — 350,000 lay leaders, both men and women, serving as chairmen of committees and directors of projects — and was reaching directly most of our millions of rural people.

Operations are carried on by the county agent, who is in all senses of the word an "educator" of his adult neighbors. He may call for special help in technical matters from the members of the staff of near-by agricultural colleges. He maintains constant contact with local problems and is a channel through which technical information is given out to groups and persons. He issues information to the daily papers through circular letters and bulletins. He talks with farmers and their wives who come to his office. And sometimes he goes to visit them in the fields or in the kitchen of the farm home. He writes letters in answer to specific questions or uses the telephone for the same purpose. He meets groups in general meetings, at demonstrations, and in special short-term

NATIONAL PUBLIC PROGRAMS

145

schools. He sets up exhibits and demonstrations. He trains
lay leaders in short courses organized for the purpose.

In the beginning, agricultural extension was generally
confined to technical matters, and the underlying purpose was to enable every farmer to produce larger and
better crops and to help farm wives to make a better
use of financial and household resources. But the program
could not be kept so simple. The prestige which came
from success in meeting obvious practical problems led
the county-extension and the home-demonstration agents
into positions of authority in their communities and exposed them to a constant fire of questions on all sorts of
professional, personal, domestic, and community matters.

The unexpected coming of a crisis, in which the problem was not to make the land produce more but to adjust
evergrowing surpluses in specific crops, such as cotton and
wheat, to a declining market and lowered prices, necessarily added still more to the duties of the extension agent.
During the life of the AAA program they were charged
with explaining the government plans to the farmers
and with enlisting the aid of all those who wanted to co-
operate in reducing production.

Even before this, however, great changes had taken
place in the extent of their responsibilities. In many
states, agricultural extension has done almost as much
to encourage drama, music, the arts, and all phases of
rural culture as it has in giving technical advice. These
agents of the counties and the agricultural colleges, spending partly local and partly national funds, are the instruments by which the whole cultural life of the small towns
and agricultural centers is being raised. The expansion
is not confined to the liberal studies. In some states,
groups for discussing current political and economic questions are flourishing under extension leadership.

The objectives of agricultural extension have run from

the narrowly technical to the widest possible service
to the entire population. All human problems lie within
the scope of the active and skillful agent. He is close to
local conditions because he is subject to local appointment.

The extension worker has behind him the well-organ-
ized resources of the federal and local governments. He is
supported in his propaganda for a better life by the
radio programs of some of the state colleges and especially by radio programs which originate in the Washington office. He can call upon specialists in almost any
branch of science or culture to bring direct teaching to
his people. Above all, he has the support of hundreds of
thousands of devoted laymen who give generously of
their time in carrying out the projects which he and
they agree upon to meet the needs of the community.

In spite of the millions of dollars which have been
appropriated for this purpose, amounting in 1935 to
$26,000,000, agricultural extension is richer in human
support than in money. The ingenuity and vision of its
leaders, both lay and professional, are more admirable
than the extent of the program.

It seems to be the consensus of opinion among people
closest to this work that future developments will turn
more and more to expansion in the liberal and cultural
arts. This is not necessarily due to any large increase
in the leisure of the farming population. In fact, some
sociologists deny that there is any more leisure on the
modern farm than there used to be. The work is of a
different kind but fully as exacting. But the farmer of
today, through print and radio and movie, finds himself
in touch with the thought and recreation of the world,
and he will not willingly forego some participation in the
things which his city brothers find pleasurable and stimulating.

Problems in farm economics appear at the present time to be those of management rather than of productive methods. The farmer is as anxious to understand world markets and the movements of financial change as he is to know how two blades of grass can be made to grow where one was growing before. In fact, he is warned rather menacingly not to grow the second blade of grass. No doubt the fundamental problem of happiness on the farm is still economic, but the other phases of life which have to do rather with the uses of income and of energy are receiving their due attention.

It is no exaggeration to say that another twenty years of active agricultural extension in America will make as profound a difference in the quality of rural life as did the work of Bishop Grundtvig through the folk schools of Denmark in the nineteenth century. To a much greater extent than most city dwellers realize, the impulses of this movement are similar to the famous Danish cultural development. The methods are more scattered, leadership is less apparently centered in a few inspired teachers, but the purposes are coming to be the same, and the results are not likely to be less.

GOVERNMENT VOCATIONAL CLASSES

The United States government carries on vocational training in co-operation with the states by authority of the Smith-Hughes law of 1917. The principal activity under this law, and the others that have amplified it, is continuation work for young men in agriculture and various trades and for girls in homemaking. The scope has broadened, however, as conditions have changed, and more attention has been paid of late to wider implications in vocational training for adults. In the report for

1934, assembled by the United States Office of Education (under whose direction the work is now being done) from all the reports of various states, it is shown that in June of that year there were nearly 370,000 men and women in agricultural, trade, and homemaking courses.

A later law (1920) has engaged the federal government and the states in rehabilitating disabled persons, and in 1934 there was a "live roll" of nearly 38,000. In addition to that live roll of persons in training, 6,319 men and 1,743 women had been rehabilitated and placed during the year.

The federal-state partnership has been on the basis of approximately one dollar of federal money for every three dollars of local money, and the total cost of vocational education and rehabilitation both, for the year ending June, 1934, was over $30,000,000.

Under the original mandate of the Smith-Hughes law, the policies of vocational schools were rather narrowly determined, but later modifications have made it possible for vocational workers in the various states to be directly helpful in meeting the unemployment problem. The active teachers, through long experience and knowledge of the occupational patterns of their communities, have become valued advisers of workers and employers. They have helped with various recovery and relief agencies "in formulating plans for emergency relief educational programs, in organizing specific training programs, and in reorganizing established vocational programs, state and local, to adapt them to the emergency situation." [1] They have also helped to strengthen the morale of the unemployed by keeping them interested in the maintenance of their skills and trade knowledge.

The experience of these workers bears out the conten-

---

[1] *Digest of Annual Reports of State Boards of Vocational Education* (1935), U. S. Office of Education, p. 15.

tion of educators that even in times of extreme depression a very large number of the unemployed could find work if they had greater skill, and that it would be wise to give them that skill for social as well as personal profit. "To the extent that it can be attributed to the failure of the community to provide the training needed to qualify workers for employment under the rapidly changing conditions of work, unemployment must be recognized as being a responsibility of vocational education." [1]

It may be that the possible developments in government-supported vocational work are masked behind the emergency of the moment. There is, however, considerable reason for predicting that, as time goes on, vocational teachers will make more provision for the adult, not only when he is unemployed but when he comes to school seeking help in increasing his productive skill. This no doubt expands the purpose of the first legislation. For reasons which have been set forth at length elsewhere, however, it was as natural for Smith-Hughes work to become more and more an adult-education enterprise as it has been for other branches of public education to accept a larger and larger share of the social responsibility for adult growth. Further widening of the terms of the mandate may be needed later. There is no real distinction between vocational training and any other adult learning. The impulse toward self-improvement of the practical average is more likely to be shown in an urge for higher income and greater trade proficiency than in any other way, but if it becomes real education it will lead eventually out of the vocational branches into something else.

There are questions of jurisdiction and organization between the states and the federal government and among the various agencies that work in the states which

[1] *Ibid.*, p. 16.

will have to be settled, as adult education in the real sense becomes more and more the concern of all the agencies involved. In some communities now there are high schools with general adult programs, Smith-Hughes classes in vocational training, agricultural extension groups, and many private agencies, all competing for the attention of the adult student. There are good reasons, of course, why the private groups should continue to go their own way. But the public groups should find some way of bringing all their efforts into a common organized system to avoid duplication and argument over jurisdiction, and to see that earnest men and women get the best possible opportunities.

The industrial night school, which has its specially defined task, has developed further in policy and methods than have most types of evening classes. Since it is attended by both continuation students and adults, it does not come wholly within our definition of adult work, but it must be included as one of the most potent agencies that extend the range of adult capacity. What is said here applies to all kinds of vocational schools for adults, regardless of the source of their support and control.

Training for advancement on a job is a specific aim, and no night-school director should be expected to neglect it. But it may too often be taken for the only possible aim of vocational study. There has been an unfortunate tendency for some leaders in the industrial night schools, supported by Smith-Hughes funds, to assume that specific training for skills which may be used to immediate benefit is the only justifiable offering. A good deal of the sharp argument over the comparative value of useful and "cultural" education has resulted. Administrators who attempt to treat the student of a vocational subject as a human being are called "academic," while those who try efficiently to achieve a narrow vocational aim are called "materialistic." A better definition of separate purposes might have prevented misunderstandings.

Such an evening industrial school as is described, for example, in the textbook of Prosser and Bass can do its best work if it undertakes to give every student something very specific, immediately to be applied to his job, and turned as quickly as possible into practical results, preferably cash. For such a school, there is nothing unreasonable in defining subject matter as that which "applies so directly and specifically to the occupation that it has functioning value for this occupation only." [1] In other words, any material offered to a student that could possibly be used by any other student in a different occupation or even a different occupational problem is for that very reason bad teaching material. This seems at first sight almost to be saying that one is doing a disservice if he gives any student more than the student asks for. The principle, however, although overstated, has good sense behind it. If an evening industrial school is a continuation school such as the authors quoted are describing, that is if it is only a fragmentary extension of the regular and the compulsory school system, or if it is a sort of repair station to which busy workers can go for specific answers to quite definitely understood and clearly stated problems, then such an organization of subject matter and such constraints on teaching are legitimate. They may not be inspired; but they can be justified in good hard sense.

The more important phases of vocational adult education, however, are quite outside the range of this sort of training. Continuation industrial schools may have a much larger attendance than any other kind of vocational school, but that does not make them of much significance

---

[1] C. A. Prosser and M. R. Bass, *Adult Education: The Evening Industrial School*, D. Appleton-Century Co., 1930, p. 100.

in the light of our general theory of adult education. A good many hours spent by an able workman in such a school might help him on the job but would leave him quite as much in need of most types of adult education as he was before. The administrator of a vocational program may claim that he has no responsibility beyond meeting the immediate vocational problems of his class. But if he does thus abrogate his opportunity as an educator of human beings, he is merely passing those tasks on to someone else.

Division of subject matter into brief unit courses, informality and directness of teaching, extreme practicality—all advocated for industrial evening schools—are simply good method, no matter where they may be found. Industrial night schools which achieve this sort of efficiency are to be praised. The ideal vocational school for adults, however, can never be merely a merchandising center into which a student comes, orders a unit of work, pays for it, and goes out. Any vocational problem, whether it be advancement, change in status, or retraining for a new skill, should have the same power to introduce the student into a new world as does any other motivating problem. The vocational motive is as good a motive upon which to base education as any other, provided that what is based upon it is genuinely education. And it will be education if the first experiences of the student in the school lead toward continuing learning and involve, as time goes on, more and more of his whole personality.

It is doubtless true that a young man who wants to learn in an industrial evening school how to be a better garage mechanic will be dissatisfied and rightfully contemptuous if what he gets does not meet that particular need. It is very doubtful, however, that anything beyond the simplest kind of skill could be taught him by a man who knew only that skill and was interested in nothing but the student's acquisition of it. Administrators of such schools are justified in insisting that their instructors must be practical men, capable of demonstrating their own successful mastery of what they are trying to teach. But much more than a mere mechanical skill is involved in any young man's desire to be a better mechanic. The whole philosophy of good workmanship, all the implications of honor and responsibility, and a wide range of social and economic relationships between his own work and the work of the society in which he lives are necessarily involved in what he thinks about. A school that can quicken and develop his interest and lead him into these channels is giving full service. The importance of federal help in occupational adult education will depend mostly upon the general acceptance of this principle.

QUESTIONS FOR DISCUSSION

1. What are the advantages and disadvantages of federal intervention in education as it now exists? What would you advocate for the future?

2. What differences between American rural conditions and Danish rural conditions account for the differences in adult education here and in Denmark?

3. Discuss the future of rural life in America and the part that adult education may play in it.

4. Do mature years make a person an easier or a more difficult subject in vocational guidance? Explain.

5. What qualities would you look for in a teacher of a mechanical skill in adult groups? Of a verbal skill,

such as advertising or public speaking? Of accounting? Of psychology? Of history? Of a language? Explain any differences.

6. Federal and state governments have programs of education for the inmates of prisons and reformatories. Discuss the general and technical problems you would expect to find in such work.

READING REFERENCES

Kolb and Brunner, *A Study of Rural Society*, Houghton Mifflin Company, 1935.

Landis and Willard, *Rural Adult Education*, The Macmillan Company, 1933.

MacCormick, Austin H., *The Education of Adult Prisoners*, The National Society of Penal Information, 1931.

Smith and Wilson, *The Agricultural Extension System*, John Wiley and Sons, 1930.

Chapter Twelve

FEDERAL EMERGENCY PROGRAMS

THE DEVELOPMENT of the economic distress which began in 1929 has led the federal government into educational enterprises it might otherwise never have undertaken. One of these enterprises may have greater effect upon adult education in this country than anything else which has happened during the present decade. This is the decision of the Federal Relief Administration to put to work in adult-education classes some forty thousand teachers who were necessarily on the relief rolls. The other striking event in this depression era is the beginning of educational work in the Civilian Conservation Corps camps for young men, the "CCC" program.

EMERGENCY CLASSES

It is too soon to say whether the emergency program of the government in adult education, listed as it has been with relief measures and touched somewhat with politics, has been on the whole an advantage or a deterrent to the development of the whole movement. There are few facts available as to the standards applied and results attained. The policy of the federal government has been to put teachers to work in adult classes not because of any special fitness they might have for that work, or because there were any special demands for what they could do, but rather because they had a claim to be paid for public service and this appeared to be the kind of public service available to keep them busy. This is not to say that no educational effect has come out of the program nor to imply that the educational results have been small, but only to insist that *relief* not *education* has been the guiding principle from the governmental and administrative standpoint.

In most of the states, the final decisions as to eligibility of teachers, as to setting up projects, and carrying out federal instructions have rested with relief agents rather than with trained educators. The inevitable result of such a policy, which may have been necessary under the circumstances, was an extreme spottiness in the quality of the work. In some states, and in many localities in all states, work of high quality has been carried on by emergency teachers, in spite of some humiliating circumstances and with very little in the way of reward or professional advancement to look forward to. In other places, routine work has been general, and extremely inferior or careless work occasional.

Administrators who have been in touch with these teachers believe generally that the teachers have learned to enjoy working with mature minds. Many of them have expressed a desire to continue in the adult field. The reactions of the hundreds of thousands of men and women who have attended the emergency adult classes all over the country have evidently been much more mixed. It would be impossible to describe any general feeling that they have shown in response to the opportunity, except that in most cases where the work has been of reasonably good quality the students have attended consistently, and some have been grateful.

There is, however, a third element in this situation, the

general public. In places where adult education was scarcely heard of before the intervention of the government, it has in some instances become identified with depression conditions and with unemployment relief. There is obvious danger that in such places it will be thought of only as a characteristic of depression times and that there will be a strong tendency to discard it as soon as the depression, with other concomitant evils, has been brought to an end. In such places, there will doubtless be educators, students, and civic-minded citizens who have learned through the government program to appreciate the value of such work. They will doubtless try to maintain, as part of the regular civic activity of their town, some fragments at least of the adult program.

It is equally certain that there are other places in which adult education by government grant for the relief of unemployed teachers has been managed in so wise and statesmanlike a way that it has already become a natural part of the life of a community. Here the withdrawal of federal funds will result not in an attempt on the part of taxpayers to end the program forthwith, but rather in a quick rescue by the loyal support of the forward-looking people who have watched the effect of classes and other adult activities upon their fellow citizens. There is good reason to believe that the government intervention has, on the whole, pushed adult education ahead.

The clientele formed by government emergency programs has differed somewhat under different state jurisdictions. In a few places, courses have been offered only to the unemployed. This narrow conception of the possibilities of government funds has not generally prevailed, however. In most places, courses have been offered to the general public as they might be offered under any other auspices, and have been taken advantage of by

all kinds of people for diverse personal needs. The more
informal part of government work, such as forums, lecture series, experiments in music, drama, and the arts,
have appealed widely. In theory, at least, the clientele
of government classes has been the whole adult population.

The government objective, as has been stated, was in
theory not educational at all. The need was not defined
in terms of clients; it was "made work" for unemployed
teachers. It would be unfair to the fact, however, to
define the objective in these terms, because the actual
programs have gone so far beyond the relief limitation.
Rather it should be said that the objective of the federal
program has been all-inclusive of the purposes which
adult education in general can embrace.

For similar reasons, it would be impossible to discuss
formally the administration, personnel, finance, and control of these government programs. They are not permanent, at least they are not expected to last, and the
administrative principles guiding them have frequently
been changed for political and relief reasons, not often
for educational reasons.

A number of efforts have been made, partly on government funds, partly on private grants, to give in-service
training to the teachers engaged. Summer institutes have
been held and a supervisory system established to maintain standards. All efforts to better the program have
naturally been handicapped by uncertainty as to the
future. Wherever and whenever these government programs develop into permanent projects under local administration, they will be changed in several important
respects. Security of tenure may then be offered those
who are engaged. They may possibly be stimulated then
by the chance of better pay and professional advancement. The problems of personnel selection and training

will take on much the same character that they have for the teachers in any other kind of public-school work.

CCC CAMPS

The Civilian Conservation Corps camps have had, almost from their foundation, an educational program. It is even more difficult to judge than the emergency program in the public schools. Of the hundreds of thousands of young men who have been enrolled in these camps from time to time and have carried on useful work in road making, forestry, soil-erosion projects, and the like, very few have escaped mental betterment. Here again, however, the federal agency ultimately responsible for the program has not been officially interested in education as such. As the emergency teaching in the public schools has been carried on for the relief of teachers, leaving education as a more-or-less incidental by-product, so the work in the camps has been carried on to occupy the time of idle young men. The Army, which has had administrative charge, has not officially paid a great deal of attention to its educational responsibilities. These statements are not made in criticism, but only to point out an unmistakable fact.

That any camp experience properly supervised has an educative influence can scarcely be denied. Many of the young men who have spent a few months under the hardy conditions of the camp have learned lessons in orderliness and good habits that will be of value to them throughout their lives. Many of them have acquired a self-respect which otherwise they might never have reached in the uncertainties of youthful life during hard times.

The educational objectives set forth when it was decided to put an "adviser" in each camp were exceptionally intelligent.

1. To develop in each man his powers of self-expression, self-entertainment, and self-culture.
2. To develop pride and satisfaction in co-operative endeavor.
3. To develop as far as practicable an understanding of the prevailing social and economic conditions, to the end that each man may co-operate intelligently in improving these conditions.
4. To preserve and strengthen good habits of health and of mental development.
5. By such vocational training as is feasible, but particularly by vocational counseling and adjustment activities, to assist each man better to meet his employment problems when he leaves camp.
6. To develop an appreciation of nature and of country life.

In spite of fine efforts by all the advisers, from those in the camp up to the two men [1] who have been in charge of the national program, it is probable that only a few of these objectives have actually been attained. From the facts that have been made available for public study, it would appear that the most serious lack has been in the third aim, to create a better civic consciousness in these young citizens. At this point there has been inevitably a conflict of ideals between the Army and the teachers. There are military officers who would say that the qualities that go to make a good soldier also make a good member of the commonwealth. There could be no dispute about some of them, as, for example, orderliness, industry, and courage. But in a self-governing country such as ours, obedience may be a vice as well as a virtue.

[1] Dean C. S. Marsh and Howard W. Oxley.

The unquestioning docility which marks the perfect soldier is not in the character of a good citizen. Largely because of official timidity there has been a notable lack in the CCC camps of anything that would encourage the free discussion of public issues, the kind of educational experience that makes for open minds and courageous thinking. There have been exceptions, but they have been due to the personal flexibility or civic awareness of some commanding officers, or to the ingenuity of educational advisers, rather than to the policies devised by the administration in general.

In examining the clientele of the CCC camp program, we realize that they are at their best learning period. If the opportunity had been seized, several hundred thousand young men could have been given, in the middle twenties, an impetus toward further self-education that would have made them of great value in any community to which they returned. It is true, no doubt, that many of them have not been sufficiently trained in the rudiments of primary or secondary schooling to take advantage of advanced work. They have been, nevertheless, all of them, at their highest learning capacity. Whatever happens to them in the camps must necessarily affect the character of their lives thereafter. In spite of the excellent plans offered and urged by the leaders in charge of the educational program, and in spite of the excellent management and scrupulous adherence to their mandate by the Army, it must still be said that the CCC camps have been in the main an educational opportunity lost. The clientele was ripe and accessible, but the objectives were not sufficiently clear to those in ultimate control.

The educational advisers scattered through the camps have been meagerly equipped with books and materials. They have been given very little opportunity to train themselves on the job. In quality they have ranged from men of limited education to men with higher degrees and pedagogical training. Their success has been largely due to their personal qualities. What was said of the federal emergency program on this point may also be repeated for the CCC camps. If they are continued and are taken as a serious public responsibility, that is, if these experiences under guidance are made genuinely valuable to the young men enrolled, they may be in the future one of the most important phases of the national adult-education movement. Their success in nearly all purposes, only excepting the accomplishment of a genuine educational aim, is the foundation upon which complete success might be built.

THE FEDERAL GOVERNMENT IN EDUCATION

The future role of the federal government in the educational system of the United States is problematic. Local control by a local school board is an essential principle in the opinion of the average American. Even the appointment of a secretary of education in the President's cabinet has often been objected to on the ground that such a step by the federal government would lead inevitably to centralized control of the schools. Reformers have urged that such centralized control would be worth whatever it cost in local autonomy because it would bring backward areas up to a minimum national standard. Into this question we need not enter here. From the standpoint of adult education, however, considering that it is largely voluntary and self-directing, it would appear that control by the national government would be extraordinarily difficult as long as vestiges of freedom are left to the American people. The administration of agricul-

tural extension and of Smith-Hughes vocational classes
has not given much evidence of a desire on the part of
central agencies to dictate educational policy to communities.   Nor have these widely beneficent federal
works shown that in our system it is easy to gather control into central bureaus. Practically, it is necessary for
any rich and powerful government, anxious for the welfare of its citizens, to offer them educational advantages
which will make them more intelligent in the exercise
of their freedom, without binding their thinking to a
tyrannous single pattern. This may be a problem for educators of adults in the future; it can scarcely be said to
be important now.

Questions for Discussion

1. What changes in public opinion regarding adult education have come as a result of emergency programs
   in your own community?

2. What parts of the emergency program which you
   have observed should be made permanent at local
   public expense?

3. How would you account for the general success, in
   spite of their lack of pedagogical training, of the
   mechanics, artists, and other teachers of skills in the
   emergency program?   In terms of their own attitudes?
   In terms of the public's attitude toward them?

4. Would you advocate that the CCC camps should be
   permanently maintained as educational agencies?
   Explain. Could the same sort of camps be established
   for girls?

5. What would you do educationally in the camps if
   you had an unlimited budget?

READING REFERENCES

HILL, FRANK ERNEST, *The School in the Camps*, American
Association for Adult Education, 1935.
HOYT, RAY, *We Can Take It, A Short Story of the C.C.C.*,
American Book Company, 1935.

The best available material on the Emergency Education Programs in the various states is to be found in the reports of state and regional directors. Many of these have been issued in mimeograph form by the state departments of education and may be secured on request. The most important exception is the reports on work done in New York City which is reported in documents issued by the city board of education.

Chapter Thirteen

COLLEGES AND UNIVERSITIES

COLLEGE students are adult in age, but we do not include their studies in the field of adult education because getting an education is, or should be, their chief concern. It is still learning as part of the system, not "continuing learning." The faculties of our higher institutions are the source of a large part of our available teachers of adults, however. From them we must draw specialists, lecturers, and forum leaders. And the institutions themselves have taken a major initiative in the movement.

UNIVERSITY EXTENSION

University extension in America, consciously modeled on the older British movement, was first undertaken by public libraries, not by colleges. It was an attempt to bring organized college education conveniently to adults who were unable to come to college in residence. A home-education department was set up in the state of New York in 1891 and in the same year a society for the extension of university teaching was organized in Chicago. In both these early instances, it was the idea of the founders that universities and colleges should pool their resources for extension purposes, and that the actual ad-

ministrative work should be carried on either by the
state or by a society organized for the purpose. In forty
years of development the American movement has become largely an activity of individual colleges and universities, but there are still examples of the earlier type
of organization (e.g., Massachusetts).

There are now more than forty colleges, universities,
teacher-training schools, and other agencies of higher
learning doing extramural teaching, either directly or
by correspondence. It is necessary to define university
extension, however, as something more than teaching.
It does make use of nearly all the known devices for
teaching, that is, classes in charge of instructors, correspondence, lectures in series or sporadically given, radio
talks, films, and books shipped out from a central library.
But extension departments undertake also a number of
services to communities that are not related to the giving
of courses. To quote Bittner, "These undertakings include assistance in community organization, and in-
formational, advisory, and demonstration services in
economics, civics, public health, hygiene, community
recreation, music, and art."[1] As students in residence in
a college have much more at their command than the
classes and the books, so in extending colleges extra-
murally, extension services have undertaken to make the
contact between the colleges and the general public as
fruitful as possible. Special help has been given not only
to persons but also to professions and to communities as
well.

The clientele of the university extension, then, is the
general adult public. State universities and the smaller
colleges do not generally go far afield, but some of the
larger and older endowed schools carry on correspondence work all over the world.

[1] W. S. Bittner, in *Handbook of Adult Education*, p. 255.

The students in extramural and correspondence classes
in the United States number possibly three hundred
thousand. Such studies as have been made of the people
who take advantage of extension opportunities would
indicate that they are a selected group, more ambitious
and, in some degree at least, more intelligent than their
fellows. They come from practically every occupation
and every economic level. Their purposes represent as
wide a range as those of any other group of adults, but
appear to be predominantly occupational.

Most colleges are willing to count work done in extension toward a degree. Few will grant a degree entirely
for extension credits and still fewer will allow correspondence work to count in any large proportion. Most extension work is taken, nevertheless, in order to have it
count toward a degree which may be completed in
residence at the first opportunity.

Bitter battles still rage on many college campuses
among faculty members who disagree as to the comparative values of residence and extension work. Extension
students are generally believed to be more serious in
their purposes and more industrious in doing the work
assigned to them, but believers in an older tradition
insist that the intangibles of education cannot be conveyed through the mail or carried even by a distinguished
scholar into a classroom remote from the university itself.
They believe that extension study must always be a comparatively meager experience and that it should not be
recognized as college work. The end of this debate is not
likely to come for some time, and when the question has
been settled a great many other questions more important
as to the right relations between universities and the
public, as well as many questions as to the place of adult
education in the nation's intellectual life, will be solved.

It remains true that the clientele of university extension is made up of people who, on the whole, appear to do better work, as measured by scholastic standards, than the average college student.

No complete studies have been made of their motives. There are reasons to believe, however, that the largest group of patrons of extension services are teachers working toward higher professional standing and workers who are seeking practical improvement.

Outside the occupational range, the chief motive is interest in liberal studies. In a comparatively small number of cases, parent education is carried on under university-extension auspices. The development of the future is probably to be in the expansion of liberal studies and the development of extension lecturing into more courageous political and social guidance.

As the clientele of university extension comprises all kinds of adult students with the exception of the very lowest educational groups, the grossly underprivileged, the objectives of the movement are the same as those of adult education in general. The comparative value of the activity is to be judged by this strongly occupational trend and by the tendency of a large proportion of the students to measure the benefits of their work by credits toward a degree. Certainly very little university-extension study is as yet carried on for the intrinsic value of the experience. But it has been strongly conditioned by two facts.

First, it began in response to an articulate public demand and was not initiated by the universities themselves. Men and women who had never had a chance to enjoy a college education or to measure its value in their own lives asked that something like it be made available to them. An ideal of intellectual life, a faith in excellence for its own sake and in personal standards without regard to external rewards or 'recognition were not within the ken of these people who were seeking something they did not fully understand.

The other fact that has greatly limited the development of university extension as real adult education is the grudging support which it has received, not so much in college administration as from members of college faculties. The monastic ideal of education is by no means dead in American colleges. Under cover of an insistence upon high scholarly standards, a very large number of college teachers are unwilling that the institutions within whose shelter they carry on their scholarly lives shall make any attempts to serve the general public. It is obvious, of course, that graduate and professional work, or highly specialized, upper-class studies, cannot be carried on except in close association with skilled teachers. University extension has rarely pretended to make this sort of intellectual opportunity available to its patrons. But to conclude that the serious interests of the average undergraduate and the quality of his study are superior to those of the average extension student is directly contrary to the opinions of many people who have observed both groups. And some of the greatest universities have not considered it beneath their dignity to put their stores of learning and technical knowledge into public use.

The administrative management of extension work is usually in the hands of a special officer of the college who in the past has been chosen from amongst the teachers, but more recently is being selected rather as a business manager than as a scholar. The larger extension services, particularly those in the western part of the country, depend upon extensive publicity and sales campaigns. This has resulted in some instances in a still wider breach between the friends of the extension division and hostile members of the general faculty. Control has rested in the hands of the presidents and the regents or trustees, but some of the state legislatures receive special appeals for funds on behalf of the extension divisions of state universities regarded as partially independent enterprises.

In recent years extension departments have been severely criticized as money-making institutions. For the most part, such criticisms are without foundation. In the case of the private university, there is no reason why an endowment fund should be drawn upon for the support of an activity which reaches an extramural group whose relationship to the institution can never be so close as that of resident students. In theory, private colleges charge a fee for extension work which is just sufficient to pay the cost. Divisions in publicly owned institutions, such as the state universities, to which separate appropriations are made are in a different situation. It is held by some educators that the state legislature should provide funds for the adult-education work of the university as generously and willingly as for the college training of the young. There is, of course, no wide acceptance of this idea, but it is partially accepted in the sense that legislatures appropriate money for adult-education work for its own sake, as a tax-supported public service and not merely as a supplement to the regular university activity. Whether those who take extension work should pay a larger portion of the cost of their education than other students has already been discussed by implication in what was said of publicly supported adult education. The actual condition is that they do pay a larger proportion than do most other students.

Most college faculties have to be rigorously combed to find scholars who have the intellectual probity and the teaching skill to deal with extension work, but in the past a great many of the most distinguished American scholars have found refreshment in extramural teaching. Students in these classes are somewhat less likely to resent an authoritative attitude than are the members of other adult classes because of the level at which the work is carried on. But ordinary college classroom teaching is not good enough.

ALUMNI PROGRAMS

General appreciation of the worth of continued study has led in the last few years to a new idea of the responsibility of the college to its alumni. Colleges have always expected that their own alumni would be specially hospitable to their extension offerings. This idea is now carried further, however, and in a recent series of graduation addresses no less than three of the presidents of the larger universities of the country publicly announced that the duties of their institutions included lifelong stimulation and teaching service to their graduates. Institutes held on the campus for brief periods, radio programs specially directed to alumni and sometimes followed by study courses, and a great development of reading lists circulated from the university libraries have expressed this new feeling of responsibility.

The whole conception of continuing education involves also new ideas as to the proper spirit of undergraduate and professional work while the student is still a member of the college community. As long as both teachers and students think of college life as something which terminates at a "commencement," it will be difficult for any institution to recapture the attention of large numbers of graduates when once they are released from its influence, presumably with its blessing. The old phrases of graduation orations are too persistent: "Equipped for life," "This knowledge with which your Alma Mater has endowed you—" The word "commencement" too often implies that learning is something left with all childish things behind. Colleges will count in the development of adult education in proportion to their success in inculcating the ideal of lifelong intellectual development in the minds of their students while they have them under direct influence.

Another consideration of the role of the college and its alumni in this movement may be noted. It is scarcely enough for an institution of higher learning to declare its awareness of a responsibility to maintain contact with its graduates and to continue to serve them. Even the great success which has been achieved by some universities in this respect is not enough. The college has an unmistakable duty to implant in each one of its graduates a sense of responsibility to the community in which he leads his life. Having had the privilege of a college education for himself, and knowing, if that experience has been successful, the values of learning, he has a greater responsibility than other citizens for the maintenance of the learning opportunities of the whole adult population around him. Universities have a duty to their alumni, but their alumni have an equally evident duty to the public. The college of the future which plays the greatest part in the development of adult education may be the one which not only offers its resources to adult students through extension or correspondence or extramural classes, and which maintains a continuing helpful contact with its graduates, but which also develops its students into citizens keenly aware of the adult-learning possibilities and needs of their communities and willing to act as leaders in their development.

QUESTIONS FOR DISCUSSION

1. Are there any values in what is called "college life" that are a serious loss to the extension or extramural student?

2. How would you account for the fact that the average extension student is believed to do better work than the average college undergraduate?

3. Discuss the advantages and disadvantages of the three methods of carrying on extension work: by having classes for extension students in the college buildings; by sending college teachers into outside classrooms; by correspondence.

4. College extension departments have often been criticized for their alleged money-making management. Assuming that they do pay a profit to the colleges, discuss the validity of the criticism.

5. In what phases of the continuing interests of alumni groups would you expect colleges to find a chance to do useful work? (Consider the five functions in turn.)

READING REFERENCES

ALDERMAN, L. R., *College and University Helps in Adult Education*, United States Office of Education, Bulletin No. 10, 1930.

BEALS, RALPH, *Aspects of Post-Collegiate Education*, American Association for Adult Education, 1935.

BITTNER and MALLORY, *University Teaching by Mail*, The Macmillan Company, 1933.

HALL-QUEST, A. L., *The University Afield*, The Macmillan Company, 1926.

SHAW, W. B., *Alumni and Adult Education*, American Association for Adult Education, 1929.

SMITH, G. B., *Purposes and Conditions Affecting the Value and Extent of Participation of Adults in the Home Study Department of Columbia*, Bureau of Publications, Teachers College, Columbia, 1935.

Chapter Fourteen

OTHER AGENCIES

A few other agencies may be commented on briefly, as more or less typical of the many that are at work. They have rapidly developing programs; their leaders are trying to make them useful for adult education. In spite of being beset by other heavy responsibilities, their staff workers are taking on new tasks because of growing demands and a growing realization of opportunity.

It has been explained that no exhaustive account of all agencies can be given here. In the Appendix is a fairly complete list of national organizations which can be said to play a part in the movement. The activities of health societies, of recreation associations, of "character-building" institutions should be studied in their own reports. Many large corporations offer their employees liberal as well as occupational studies. It is in the nature of adult education that its purposes should be served by a wide variety of institutions, many of which have been serving the intellectual and cultural needs of mature people for years without being aware of any connection with a general movement, without, indeed, being aware that they were engaged in education. The growth of professional self-consciousness and a wider knowledge of effective methods may threaten these volunteer agencies with rigid standards, but they will also clarify their procedures. They can doubtless be depended on to maintain their vigorous initiative and individuality.

LIBRARIES

Librarians have always been teachers. All keepers of books who have been more than mere custodians have helped to educate those who came to use the stores of learning which libraries hold. But full consciousness of this responsibility for education, particularly of adults, has only recently emerged in the library world. The first bulletin on the subject was issued by the American Library Association in 1924. Two years later, the extensive report, *Libraries and Adult Education*, was published and has been the basis for professional interest in the subject. And in this field, as in so many others, what had been more or less haphazardly done suddenly became part of a professional program.

But although most librarians have come to accept some responsibility for adult education as a part of their work, it has not been possible as yet to define exactly the scope of library activity. In the first statement, the report already referred to on libraries and adult education, four chief functions were listed. These were four chief needs for effective work. First, a greater quantity of readable books; second, a better book supply for the population at large; third, better training in reading in the schools; and fourth, better organization of direct service to those who are educating themselves. None of these has been adequately met in the ten years that have elapsed since. Only one of them, however, the second, is strictly the business of librarians as such. The others are responsibilities which they share with other agencies.

Whatever else he may be, a librarian is always a person who has charge of books and who accepts responsibility for seeing that books are available to the greatest possible number of people. That this task is not yet

achieved in very large degree is shown by the report of
the Library Extension Board of the American Library
Association for the decade 1925–35.[1] This report states
that only 63 per cent of the people in America are at the
present time provided with library service, in spite of the
great gains achieved in that decade. The number of
people who have public library books within reach grew
from more than sixty million to more than seventy-seven
million. There are still 45,130,093 people, however, who
cannot get books from any public source. Most of these
citizens who are without what we have come to take
as a normal part of the equipment for living are in
rural areas. In fact, about three quarters of all the people
who live outside the cities are denied library help. The
development and equalization of library services remains
the primary task for the librarian in adult education.
All agencies are handicapped when they attempt to work
with people who have an inadequate book supply. The
librarian is a foundation element in any adult-education
program because his energies go to building what is basic
to the work of everyone else, the supply of books.

Where books are available, librarians are guides to
reading. They have always been willing to put their own
knowledge of books at the service of inquirers, but this
advisory function has become much more highly organized in the last few years. The "readers' adviser," a
librarian specially trained to consult personally with
patrons, is becoming a familiar figure in the library
lobby or reading room.

The third function of the librarian is to take his own
part in stirring the intellectual curiosity of people who
come to him as readers of books, and also to use the public
library as the place from which can go out the kind of
propaganda that arouses public interest in ideas. In

---

[1] *Bulletin of the American Library Association*, June, 1935, p. 324.

other words, the librarian has a duty to urge both individuals and communities toward greater intellectual activity and wider interests.

It should be understood, of course, that these three functions are those of the librarian in his professional capacity. It often happens that a librarian, because of superior education and more alert mind, is also a leader in community thinking. There are many instances of this educational leadership. Librarians have been accepted as the initiators of adult-education programs quite apart from the fact that in their services as librarians they would, in any case, serve any program that any other leader might be able to get under way.

The second professional function, that of guidance, has become specialized in the readers' advisory service. Among members of the profession there is still some dispute as to the advantage of having people definitely trained as readers' advisers instead of having every person on the staff feel it is his responsibility to help anyone who asks a question. The tendency unquestionably is toward specialization. By 1935 there were some sixty-three professional readers' advisers at work in forty-four American public libraries.

These educators must have tact and genuine human sympathy and, in the opinion of competent professional people, they must be good librarians. That is, they must know books and the management of books.

The education carried on by the readers' adviser is usually on the basis of a considerable personal knowledge of the student, and is more truly worthy of the name than much that is done by public lecturers and by others who hand out prepared doses of educational material with no regard for the particular need of any consumer. A readers' adviser must attempt to diagnose the educational needs of anyone who comes to consult him.

Lacking the authority and the advantages of an acknowledged teacher, he needs more understanding and
tact for this diagnosis than is elsewhere required. Having
estimated immediate needs, he suggests or prepares a
list of the readings which he thinks will be satisfactory.
In the best services the adviser tries to maintain continuous personal contact with the reader so that unexpected obstacles and widening interests can be taken
care of. He often maintains an up-to-date list of all the
educational opportunities of the city. A readers' adviser
is a teacher who cannot make a class of his students because each one has distinct and different problems. He
cannot be sure that a list of books prepared for an inquirer in a particular subject on one day will be of any
use to another inquirer who asks about the same subject
on another. He must be a shrewd judge of people and a
sound judge of the progressive educational values of
literature. And his genuinely educational help is very
often misunderstood and received without thanks by
the beneficiary.

While this specialized service does what it can for the
individual, the general activity of the public library and
its staff in stimulating the reading of the community
works upon a broader scale and with broader methods.
All of the devices of publicity are used by modern
workers, window displays, not only of books but of interesting illustrative things, book reviews presented at
organization meetings, book talks over the radio, arrangements of new books in which a beneficent cunning
tempts the passerby.

In modern libraries, there is a growing tendency to
scatter books away from central collections so that the
actual physical presence of reading material will make
itself felt in unexpected places. The great central monu-
mental library is, no doubt, a necessary part of library

systems, but branches scattered in convenient places and even, as in some highly developed state and county systems, small deposits of books in places that are really not libraries at all, and traveling book trucks, are ways of bringing books and readers face to face.

A further extension of leadership by the library which goes beyond the exhibition and the lecture hall is the provision of discussion groups for library patrons. This latest development is based upon realization of the fact that people can read without thinking. Most people appear to have as great a need to talk about ideas as to acquire them from print. Librarians, recognizing this need, have in many places encouraged groups to meet in the assembly rooms, either informally or at stated periods under appointed leaders. These groups are similar to discussion groups described elsewhere in this book, and they are mentioned here only because the library as an institution has certain special advantages in providing both the meeting place and the special reading matter without which a discussion group is not likely to be successful. And it is entirely likely that in the future a great deal of informal discussion will become a part of the normal service of the library to the public.

No extensive adult-education program, whether supported by public funds and carried on through public agencies, or as the work of private agencies, can be done in a community which lacks a fully developed consciousness of public-library needs and a well-established public-library foundation. This fundamental position of the library will not be changed. As time goes on, it is extremely likely, in the opinion of most of those who have watched developments, that the librarian will be more and more active in the general development of adult education and will take on further functions in the program's operation.

The public library is like the public school: it is open to everybody. Its aim is the highest that an institution can have, disinterested public service. In two generations, public libraries have established a tradition of administration without political interference that is unique among tax-supported agencies. "Librarianship" is a profession. How its members should be trained is a technical matter, but the educator may venture the hope that methods and principles of adult education will some day be part of their required study. Success in this field can no longer be measured in mere circulation figures. The intangible but real pulsations of thinking among the people of a town are the measure of the public library's achievement as an agency of adult education.

MUSEUMS

The museum as an agency in adult education has for its clientele the whole population of all ages and kinds. It can accommodate whole families together as learning groups and has an added social importance on that account. But it must be something more than a mere collection of curious objects to be idly visited on a Sunday afternoon. A collection of materials, records, and rare objects may be useful to scholars and in the advance of science, but not count for much in popular education. The teaching museum is not a passive guardhouse full of treasure; it is a center of activities in which the collections are only the materials to be used. Pioneers of imagination and daring have shown that the real work is in teaching the diverse and irregular clientele that comes within the agency's reach.

It would be too much to say that all or even most of the museums in this country have become teaching centers. Many of them have educational departments which are excellent as adjuncts to the visual education work of the public schools, but too often the displays and labeling and incidental lecturing are on such a plane of routine custodianship that very little value is got from the treasures the museums possess.

A few leading institutions have shown the way. By thinking of themselves as adult-education centers, and by marshaling every known device for the better exploitation of their collections, they have conveyed information and aroused thought. The alert curator can do more than merely invite people into the presence of interesting or beautiful things. He can sometimes by means of helpful labels teach things not found in books. By the arrangement of objects, he gives a sense of history and of continuous development in some element of culture that is more vivid and more convincing than can be got by any other means. He can offer the proof of scientific conclusions in ways that mere words can never accomplish. Museums are highly concentrated extensions of man's environment, and when intelligently managed they do much more than supplement other forms of study or teaching. They create educational values of their own. The objectives of the museum are no more limited than is its circle of patrons. They include all the educational aims that can be attained in informal ways.

The administration of a good museum involves three kinds of skill that may not appear compatible. They are: (a) scientific research, (b) teaching, and (c) what may be called housekeeping. The great museum collections vie with the great universities in providing the materials for scientific research and in carrying on difficult investigations. Out of the accumulations, constantly renewed and added to, must be selected those materials which by case display, by use in lectures, by reproduction, and by circulation to other centers will accomplish the teaching purposes of the institution. A good museum is one to which people constantly return, not only to repeat experiences, but in the certainty of finding new ones. The things must also be taken care of and the person who has them in his charge is a host to the visiting public. Scientist, teacher, housekeeper.

Most museums in the United States are public institutions, but many are under private control and financed by private endowment. The tendency is for great collections to pass eventually into the ownership of the municipality or state. Institutional personnel has in the past been recruited by apprenticeship methods. Universities are beginning to establish courses for the training of curators and assistants. These training courses have to do, naturally, more with other phases of museum work than with teaching. For teaching in a museum, that is, for arranging visual materials so that they will have the greatest effect, for lecturing and for all the informal work, two things are needed. These are: first, a thorough knowledge of the material which is being used; second, acquaintance with the methods of adult education.

The programs of active museums embrace a great many things which are not different when carried on under their auspices from what they are in the program of a public school or of any other institution. They may give lectures or "gallery talks" on subjects which their collections can be used to illustrate. They may direct "walks" for informal nature study. They may produce books based upon their own materials or their own investigations. These things are subject to all the comments which may be made on similar activities elsewhere. The essential work of the museum, however, which is the use of visual material for teaching on the most informal level, is an art in itself.

RELIGIOUS BODIES

Churches of all denominations and the young people's societies attached to them have engaged in general adult education progressively in the last decade, developing their programs naturally out of the religious adult education which has always been one of their primary activities. In spite of the steady trend toward secularization of denominational colleges in this country, churches maintain that their special religious opinions give them special responsibilities toward their members. Churches and societies of the Roman Catholic and Hebrew faiths have worked mostly within their own membership. The Young Men's Christian Association and the Young Women's Christian Association, being of a somewhat more public secular character and less denominational, have offered learning opportunities to all comers. Most churches and religious groups have some degree of local freedom in such matters, and the educational programs have been very different in different places, depending largely upon what other agencies were trying to do and upon the institutional progressiveness of each group. From the standpoint of those professionally concerned with adult education, it is important to note that the field of these religious agencies is still not clearly defined.

The claim has been made for some of them that they are specially charged with educating the whole adult population.[1] But it is obvious that if any of them, or all of them together, are to attack the whole problem of adult education they must be endowed with resources and trained teachers far beyond anything now within their scope. With due respect for their high-minded pur-

[1] Thomas H. Nelson, *Adult Education for Social Needs*, The Association Press, 1933, pp. 63 and 70.

poses and admiration for their great achievements, one may still question whether adult education will be dominated by religious bodies at a time when all the rest of education has a progressively less and less religious character. This, of course, is not in any sense a comment upon the necessary function which such religious bodies perform in relation to their religious doctrines, which is (to use the Roman-Catholic phrase) "propaganda" for their beliefs, but only to point out that even the greatest and most powerful of religious bodies are only partly representative of the general public.

If, instead of taking on a larger burden, each religious body, or young people's society, works for its own constituency, an exact definition of program will not be so necessary. The program of the Young Women's Hebrew Association, for instance, may on this basis well be whatever the special constituency of the Young Women's Hebrew Association demands, limited naturally by the resources of that institution. These constituencies are gathered together mostly for other than educational reasons.

Many agencies serve a larger public on an activity basis as, for example, the Young Men's Christian Association, with its approximately one million members and an additional number half as large who participate in various programs, many of which are educational. But for the most part the principle holds, special services to a special group, the size of which is determined by the attractiveness of the program somewhat, but more profoundly by the essential appeal of the institution's religious point of view.

In special service to a special constituency there are both dangers and advantages. The danger is that, since the institution is not responsible to the public, its educational standards will be low. The advantage is that there will be a certain degree of social cohesion which will make for effectiveness in the program, and that in most cases it will be possible to appeal to moral and sectarian motives which will re-enforce the motives that bring the average adult into a public high school or lecture hall.

Many questions as to what part these agencies can take in developing the field remain. Whether they will be decided by the institutions themselves or by consultation with unaffiliated educational experts may to some extent determine the answers. The four most evident of these questions are as follows:

First, how far does the "point of view" of each institution color its actual teaching, and how far should it influence educational activity? Churches of every sect, young people's associations, and all of the other organizations which may be classified in this group have expressed points of view from which they regard the world and its problems. In some cases, it is clearly defined in a creed. In others, interpretation is left to the conscience of individual members, but it is nonetheless insisted upon in all statement of policy. Doubtless the point of view will weigh more in the consideration of some subjects than of others. But it is not yet defined, in terms which the professional educator can understand, just what is to be the relation, in the developing adult-education activities of these agencies, between a certain "point of view" and general social and scientific problems.

The *second* question is this: How far should an agency which represents a creed go in offering educational opportunities to the whole community in which it is situated? What reasons has it for going outside its own membership? In most conferences on matters of policy of this sort the only questions discussed are those as to the "need" of the public. But listing all the needs of the community in which it happens to work does not define the program of any institution. Other elements which must necessarily come fully into consideration are: the existence of other institutions, their resources as compared with those of the agency making plans, the adequacy of its own resources in face of problems which might be attacked, the advisability of taking on work which can be met in part but not fully with given resources, and a number of other points involving one major question.

This major question has to do with the over-organization of American community life. A great many things which need to be done, among which are included the aims of adult education, fail to get done because too many agencies, guided by high-minded but institutionally ambitious people, spread their strength over too wide a program. An agreed-upon division of labor would frequently increase the effectiveness of the total work done by all the co-operating agencies. This might interfere with their institutional growth, and that may be the chief reason why co-operation is so seldom achieved. Religious bodies are, of course, no more prone to this institutional ambition than are those of any other sort. But they are not free of it.

The *third* general question is, How far can each agency assume a share of the responsibility for leading the community as a whole toward a general program of adult learning? This is obviously related to the second question; and it has already been mentioned as one of the present policies still undecided in regard to public libraries.

Since the educational programs of all of these religious and partly religious agencies involve more and more a study of current problems, how far are their educational programs to include institutional commitments to social action? This is the *fourth* question. Some denominations, as such, take official positions upon social issues and expect of their adherents a loyal agreement. Few announce ruthlessly defined principles and undertake to swing the whole social power of their membership as a bloc.

This is closely related to the first question but is slightly different in fact. It involves more than a color or trend given to teaching because of "point of view." We are concerned now with the extent to which these religious bodies take action in social crises and how far their educational programs are to be used for the building up of the body of adherents who are loyal to this program of action and consider themselves bound morally and intellectually to support the institution, in conflict if necessary. The official literature of the religious bodies and the churches, and the publicly expressed opinions of major leaders have not as yet provided an answer to this question in regard to most of the institutions. Indeed, no religious body of wide influence in this country takes a fixed and positive stand in regard to matters of political decision or of social action except in rare instances. The opposition of the Catholic Church to birth control and the generally prohibitionist attitude of one group of Protestant Christian churches are examples of extreme institutional action.

In the social sciences, however, subjects are constantly passing in and out of the focus of immediate importance. The swift changes of today may at any moment make action necessary. The Young Women's Christian Association, as one example, contents itself with the announcement of national policies which are not more than principles adhered to by nationally elected representatives. Local associations follow or not as they please.

The working out of the relationship between this need for institutional decisiveness and a general educational program is a matter of great importance for the future.

As the position of religious bodies in our present folkways is uncertain, so must their programs of education waver until definition has been achieved.

WORKERS' GROUPS

Workers' education is carried on by special agencies working with a special clientele. In this, its activity resembles somewhat that of the churches, since the constituencies are already in existence. Educational opportunities are offered to members of unions or trade groups among other membership services, and they are expected to take part in them as one among other expressions of loyalty to an institution. Workers' education, in the sense of programs devised for underprivileged wage earners, has been the primary function of adult classes in Great Britain and in some other countries. In America, the term is applied mostly to programs organized by groups of wage earners according to their own conception of what they need. Programs of this self-directed character have been carried on by the Workers' Education Bureau of America, closely affiliated with the American Federation of Labor, by a number of schools in special summer sessions, particularly for women in industry, by unions co-operating with extension divisions of universities, and most widely by labor unions for their own members.

In the past, workers' education has been concerned with the first of the five functions of the adult movement, remedial education, and still more with political education. It has attempted to bring the members of working groups up to the plane of effective social participation and has in nearly all cases embodied a program of action in its educational offerings. This allies it with certain types of "party" political schools for adults which are the

expression of definite attitudes toward the social order
and its possible improvement.

There is reason to believe from recent events that the
students in these workers' programs are beginning to ask
for more studies of a liberal nature. With no less interest in the fundamental motives which bring all mature persons into educational activity, that is a desire to
improve their own status in the world or to make the
world like their own ideal, they are seeking ways of enjoying things for their own sake. They want to live better
day by day in the long campaign for social betterment.
This need not dull the other more pragmatic motives.
The work should be more effective for all purposes if the
offerings are richer and more varied.

There remains, however, a fundamental dispute between two groups of practitioners in this field. Some believe that their purpose should be to bring the widest
possible educational opportunity to workers, giving them,
according to their interest, the same things that would
be given to any other clientele. The other group believe
in a class-conscious program. The leaders seek, more or
less, through workers' education to bring the industrial
employees of the country into a coherent and, eventually,
into a politically effective bloc. This fundamental cleav-
age, in theory and in practice, is not exactly the same as
the difference dividing the radical from the conservative
thinkers who are engaged with labor problems, but to a
large extent the more radical tend to adhere to the second
idea.

If the fundamental principles offered in this essay led
to a sympathy with the second principle, that is to the
conviction that workers should be treated as a separate
class, made conscious of their separateness, and equipped
to attain power as a group, it would be necessary to go to
considerable length in discussing workers' education and

its techniques. Our general philosophy, however, does not admit of such a conclusion. It leads rather to the principle that everything in this book applies in some degree to workers' education as it applies to any other form of adult learning. Workers as members of the community have the same reasons for wanting improved intellectual conditions as other people have, and will attain them by the same processes and through the same agencies, whether they set up the agencies for themselves or use their share of what is offered to the whole social community.

PARENT-TEACHER ASSOCIATIONS

The Parent-Teacher movement has realized its adult-education possibilities only in one direction, parent education. Its usefulness in helping to develop and support that phase has been very great, however, and it promises to be still greater in the future. As long as parent education is largely a "folk" movement and depends upon lay leaders for widely extended effectiveness, parent-teacher councils are the natural framework for the co-operative effort of professionals and parents in applying scientific understanding to everyday relational problems.

The councils are becoming truly educational in their work among their own members. In the beginning, some years ago, much of the "education" which they fostered was little more than a combination of charity toward the schools and unwise interference. The building up of child-study classes led by lay leaders gave them a purpose in keeping with their original ideas of possible usefulness. It stimulated deeply their own intellectual life. There have been some few experiments which took the members still further into general self-education. Parent-teacher groups are as well, or almost as well, adapted for the study of social and political problems as they are for studying the special problem of the adjustments between generations. The Parent-Teacher Association council is not exactly a women's club although it is made up usually of women. Some of the disadvantages of the ordinary women's club, in which social congeniality may be allowed to outweigh intellectual parity, are absent. Active discussions are frequent in the parent-teacher councils, where mothers, and sometimes—miraculously—a few fathers, gather together because their children are undergoing similar school experiences. Such a council provides a wider variety of experience and interests than a women's club is likely to offer, and for some purposes is a better nucleus for a study group.

The fundamental motives which will inspire P.T.A. members to pursue learning outside their responsibility as mothers and fathers and teachers are, of course, not different from the motives which originally brought them together. Better parenthood implies development of the mature person as a personality and as a citizen. A fully responsible parent cannot well dodge his duty to develop all his powers and all his social relationships to their fullest value. The quality of his own life and the atmosphere of his own intellectual activity will necessarily condition the opportunities of his children. Parent-Teacher Associations are in a strong position to develop this motive for the general learning activity of all their members, not to neglect the primary questions of family life, but to expand to more impersonal, communal relationships, and finally to all varieties of intellectual interest.

Questions for Discussion

1. Discuss the educational activities (outside of service to school children) of the public library in any community that you know. How much are they limited by the qualities of the library personnel? By lack of funds? By lack of public appreciation?

2. Make a visit to any available museum. Discuss your own experience. What caught your attention? How much of your interest in the exhibits was due to your interest in subject matter and how much to artfulness of display? Did you learn anything that could not have been better learned from books?

3. What are the advantages and disadvantages of a religious creed as a basis for an educational program? Are the advantages greater if the basis is not a strict creed but a general designation such as "Christian," or "Hebrew"?

4. It is said that workers' classes are turning more toward liberal subjects. Can you explain?

5. Which of the agencies not commented upon in full in this book would you consider most important?

Reading References

American Library Association, *Libraries and Adult Education*, The Macmillan Company, 1926.

Andrus, Ruth, *Discovering Lay Leadership in Parent Education*, The University of the State of New York Press, 1935.

Chancellor, John, *A.L.A. Board on the Library and Adult Education: Report 1924-34*, A.L.A. Bulletin, June, 1935.

Coleman, Laurence V., *Recent Progress and Condition of*

Museums, Bulletin No. 20, United States Office of Education, Chap. XXII, 1931.

HANSOME, MARIUS, *World Workers' Educational Movements*, Columbia University Press, 1931.

HUDSON, CYRIL E., *The Teaching Church: Methods in Adult Religious Education*, The Macmillan Company, 1933.

NELSON, THOMAS H., *Ventures in Informal Adult Education*, Association Press, 1933.

REA, P. M., *The Museum and the Community*, Science Press, 1932.

SMITH, HILDA W., *Women Workers at the Bryn Mawr Summer School*, American Association for Adult Education, 1929.

Chapter Fifteen

WHAT CAN WE EXPECT?

THE ADULT-EDUCATION movement has organized and given reality to some of the impulses that make for social progress. If it continues to develop, it will some day be one of the most effective of such institutions because it aims to improve the human material with which progress can be built. A solid conviction as to its value and its potential power in human affairs does not enable us, however, to prophesy. It is not new in civilization, as we have seen, and similar movements have risen only to fall back again, ended by inertia or catastrophe. It may be possible at the present time to predict this much: In America, adult education is likely to gather momentum for some time to come.

The acceleration of social change gives no sign that it is about to slow down. Problems do not get simpler, although the temptation to reduce their painful complexity to simple terms grows upon us. A rational skepticism in the face of propaganda is more and more difficult, and for that reason is more necessary. We may be thankful that the desire for learning grows by being satisfied.

We have already pointed out that our population is older with each generation because the birth rate is going down and the average life is longer. There are, even now, a few communities that have school equipment larger than their children can make full use of. Will they now use this equipment for older people in order to get the benefit of their investment? In any case, there will be profound social and educational changes in a society that is made up of more mature citizens.

It is also true that, except for the temporary setback of the present time, we are likely to go on raising the general educational level. Whether we shall ever again have as many students in colleges and universities as we had in 1929 may be a question. But that we shall go ahead at least toward a high-school level for everybody is almost certain. The natural result of a more general educational interest will be a greater demand for adult education. For reasons which should have been made clear before this, an American people that is both older and better educated will demand more opportunities for continuing to learn.

The character of this future adult education is much more difficult to speculate about. Much will depend upon the continued life of our democratic social and political structure. If America undertakes its own experiment with a totalitarian philosophy (which to this one observer seems extremely unlikely), there will still be adult education, but it will bear little resemblance to that which has been described and advocated in this book. European countries that have ventured on totalitarian and tyrannic experiments in government have all been logical enough to work out the same philosophy of education for their mature citizens as they have had for their children. They have not lacked adult education. They have not neglected the minds of their men and women. They have, it may go without saying, completely neglected the kind of adult education we are speaking of here, since we have urged above all other things freedom to learn.

No state which is risking its future upon a single social

or political philosophy, no matter how sincere or how sound that philosophy may be, can grant the luxury of free thinking to its citizens. Modern dictatorships are not like the dictatorships of old, mere mechanical infliction of a tyrannous violence on a helpless people. The modern dictator, Communist, Fascist, Nazi, or whatnot, takes possession first of the organs of public opinion and solicits the support of his people and their good will by providing that no questionable or critical truths get to their attention. If America goes through such a phase, adult education will be the preachment of the "adult" version of the official dogma.

There are other shifts and changes possible in American philosophy, however, which may affect the working out of the impulses now finding their expression in adult-education activities. There is still bitter dispute as to the qualities and capacities of men, and as to the efficiency of the measures by which we judge them in the laboratory of the psychologist or in practical life. Leaders in this field, of whom Thorndike[1] is one, have advocated a concentration of our resources upon those selected students of whose capacity we think we can be sure. Others push to the extreme of saying that intrinsic quality is all that counts and that training can do nothing with the inferior human material. Still others go to the opposite extreme of saying that environment is all and that education is only opportunity. Without taking part in so vexed and eternal a question, we may say, in accord with the philosophy that has supported all the principles set forth in this essay, that whatever may be the differences among men and the sons of men, there are still too many injustices in environment for us to be sure that everyone has had a chance. When environment has been suffi-

[1] E. L. Thorndike, *Adult Interests*, D. Appleton-Century Co., 1935, Chap. X.

ciently perfected so that we can be quite sure that no genius is lost and no talent sacrificed, when we can be certain that everyone has had a chance to show his quality, then it may be time to start paring down our opportunities. That time seems a long way off.

It is costly, certainly, to offer learning opportunities to millions of men and women. It has been costly to offer those opportunities to many more millions of boys and girls. But it would take a hardy pessimist to say that there have not been gains, measurable and overwhelmingly sufficient, in return for our generosity to the oncoming generations. The complex and hazardous civilization by which we live would be quite impossible except for the developed brains of millions of young people who under any less generous educational system would have been shut out from development. Much of the money has been wasted, no doubt. But still more should be spent before we can be sure that we are not being niggardly to our own cost. The extent to which this principle can be applied to adult education will be a matter of future thought. It seems unlikely that we will err in the direction of too much. Even our democratic society is likely to be fearful about getting a fair return for its investment. The basic philosophy of this book has been that a person's right to further learning is determined by his desire for it. If we can continue to meet what will probably be a constantly growing desire, we shall still not be undertaking too much, because only then can we be sure that rare and valuable qualities will not be lost.

There are signs of new kinds of social thinking in America, new types of consciousness, new impulses toward co-operation. Adult education is only one of the ways by which all the resources of a social group may be put to work for the betterment of life. But it is important because it has to do with the life of the mind. It undertakes to quicken and inform, to sharpen native powers, to match intelligence against besetting evils, and to sustain the hope of constant growth. No social institution has a higher secular aim or a more difficult task. Our success in managing our difficult civilization may hang upon the use we make of the learning power which is ours as long as we are alive.

APPENDIX

NATIONAL ORGANIZATIONS

The following list of organizations includes most of those which are active in the field of adult education. Many other agencies contribute something to the general effort toward stimulating the mental lives of men and women, but they have been omitted from this list either because their adult-education work is a minor phase of their operations or because they are commercial. The educational influence of commercial agencies is often of the highest significance, but these agencies have been excluded from the scope of this volume.

American Alumni Council
  University of North Carolina, Chapel Hill, N. C.

American Association for Adult Education
  60 East 42 Street, New York, N. Y.

American Association of Museums
  Smithsonian Institution, Washington, D. C.

American Association of University Women
  1634 Eye Street N. W., Washington, D. C.

American Country Life Association
  105 East 22 Street, New York, N. Y.

American Library Association
  520 North Michigan Avenue, Chicago, Ill.

Association of the Junior Leagues of America, Inc.
  Hotel Waldorf-Astoria, New York, N. Y.

Chautauqua Institution
  Chautauqua, New York

Child Study Association of America
  221 West 57 Street, New York, N. Y.

Foreign Language Information Service
  222 Fourth Avenue, New York, N. Y.

Foreign Policy Association
  8 West 40 Street, New York, N. Y.

General Federation of Womens Clubs
  1734 N Street N. W., Washington, D. C.

National Advisory Council on Radio in Education
  60 East 42 Street, New York, N. Y.

National Catholic Welfare Conference
  1312 Massachusetts Avenue N. W., Washington, D. C.

National Commission on the Enrichment of Adult Life
  1201 Sixteenth Street N. W., Washington, D. C.

National Committee on Education by Radio
1201 Sixteenth Street N. W., Washington, D. C.

National Congress of Parents and Teachers
1201 Sixteenth Street N. W., Washington, D. C.

National Council of Parent Education
60 East 42 Street, New York, N. Y.

National Education Association
1201 Sixteenth Street N. W., Washington, D. C.

National Federation of Business and Professional Womens Clubs
1819 Broadway, New York, N. Y.

National Home Study Council
839 Seventeenth Street N. W., Washington, D. C.

National League of Women Voters
726 Jackson Place, Washington, D. C.

National Recreation Association
315 Fourth Avenue, New York, N. Y.

National University Extension Association
Indiana University, Bloomington, Indiana

Workers Education Bureau of America
1440 Broadway, New York, N. Y.

Young Men's Christian Associations of the United States
347 Madison Avenue, New York, N. Y.

Young Men's Hebrew Association and Young Women's Hebrew Association
Organized under Jewish Welfare Board, 220 Fifth Avenue, N. Y.

Young Women's Christian Associations of the United States
600 Lexington Avenue, New York, N. Y.

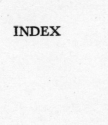

INDEX